# Collected Parodies

# Works by J. C. Squire

VERSE

POEMS. First Series. 2ND EDITION
POEMS. Second Series
THE BIRDS AND OTHER POEMS
THE MOON: A Poem
THE MOON. Special Limited Edition de Luxe

PARODIES

COLLECTED PARODIES. 2ND EDITION
TRICKS OF THE TRADE. 8TH EDITION

PROSE

LIFE AND LETTERS
THE GOLD TREE
BOOKS IN GENERAL. By Solomon Eagle. 3RD EDITION
BOOKS IN GENERAL. Second Series. By Solomon Eagle
BOOKS IN GENERAL. Third Series. By Solomon Eagle

# Collected Parodies

By J. C. Squire

Hodder & Stoughton
Limited

*Printed wholly in England for the* MUSTON COMPANY.
*By* LOWE & BRYDONE, PRINTERS, LTD., PARK STREET, CAMDEN TOWN, LONDON, N.W.1

CONTENTS

# PREFACE

THIS collection includes almost the whole of three previous books : "Imaginary Speeches," "Steps to Parnassus" and "Tricks of the Trade," which contain all the parodies I have ever published or, I imagine, ever shall publish. For permission to reprint from the first two I am indebted to Messrs. Allen and Unwin. Some of the parodies have been re-grouped ; a few have been omitted. I was not quite sure what to do about the "Imaginary Speeches" in which I endeavoured to exhibit the mannerisms of mind and language of a number of politicians who were prominent in 1909, when they were written. The speeches dealt with a hypothetical future which will not now exist. They mentioned persons no longer conspicuous. They treated problems which have been either shelved or partially solved : one, for instance, visualized women's suffrage coming under conditions very different from those which saw its achievement. I have, therefore, compromised by reprinting three only of them in the hope that, as some readers, when they first appeared, found them interesting as topical criticism, so others may now find them interesting as recalling "the world before the war."—J.C.S.

I

## M. MAURICE MAETERLINCK

## PELISSIER AND MARIANE

[SCENE. *A glade in an ancient forest. The trees have vast trunks. Over and through them* (L.) *one can dimly see the crown of a ruined tower. Its stones are massive, and it has been inhabited, but is so no longer. It is evening.* PELISSIER *and* MARIANE *stand by the bole of a great tree, melancholy and silent, gazing at the last light. He is of robust build, and she clings to him for support. Both are pale with that mysterious pallor that lives in moonbeams when a cloud half covers the surface of the moon.*

MARIANE. Pélissier ! [*A wind shakes the branches and the leaves rustle.*] Pélissier ! . . . It is a little wind ! . . . Did you not hear it, Pélissier ?

PELISSIER. Yes, Mariane, it is a little wind, a child wind. Perhaps it has lost its way in the world. We, have we lost our way, Mariane ?

MARIANE. Pélissier ! . . .

PELISSIER. Yes, I think we have lost our way. . . . I dreamt last night that I was walking, walking amid the meshes of an enormous net of bushes and plants which sucked and throttled me so that I could hardly breathe. . . . And you, you were there too, Mariane. I could hear you somewhere making little cries, the cries I have often heard you make when you have found some wounded thing : some bird, perhaps, that the cruel cat has been tormenting. . . .

MARIANE. Pélissier! . . .

PELISSIER. I think that in my dream we were wandering there for ever.

MARIANE. Pélissier! . . .

[*It has grown darker. The moon has not yet risen, but the tower and the other objects are still faintly visible in a diffused bluish light, like the light of infinity. For a space* PELISSIER *and* MARIANE *are silent. Slowly, over the farthest trees, the moon rises. The tower becomes a pillar of black and silver, and a pure and brilliant ray strikes* PELISSIER *and* MARIANE.

PELISSIER. Hush, Mariane!

MARIANE. Pélissier!

PELISSIER. Do you not see them?

MARIANE. Who, Pélissier? . . . Oh, I am afraid . . . Oh, I am cold!

PELISSIER [*his voice is low and level and brooding, and his eyes are fixed and sorrowful*]. They are over there, over behind that tree. They are coming this way. Do you not see them? It is the six old men whom we saw yesterday by the place where the old king lived.

MARIANE. Oh, Pélissier! Oh, I see them! Oh, they are horrible! I think I must have known them long ago. . . . I think I must have known them before I was born!

[*From the forest on the left* SIX OLD MEN *enter. The five of them are blind and deaf and dumb, but the sixth is not dumb. He is only blind and deaf. They walk very slowly and stumblingly. The first feels his way with his staff. The others also feel their ways with their staffs, tripping over sticks and dead leaves as they go.*]

THE FIRST OLD MAN. Moo! [*He enters the wood on the right.*]

THE SECOND OLD MAN. Moo! [*He enters the wood on the right.*]

THE THIRD OLD MAN. Moo. [*He enters the wood on the right.*]

THE FOURTH OLD MAN. Moo! [*He enters the wood on the right.*]

THE FIFTH OLD MAN. Moo! [*He enters the wood on the right.*]

THE SIXTH OLD MAN. Ah! . . . I think God must be dead to-night. . . . [*He stumbles.*] Blast! [*He enters the wood on the right.*]

PELISSIER. Did you hear what the sixth old man said, Mariane?

MARIANE [*vaguely, as one in a dream*]. Oh! . . . There is a child there . . . over where the old king lived. . . . . It is blue. . . . It is blue like the night! . . . I do not know why it is blue! . . . Oh, I am afraid!

PELISSIER. He said that he thought God must be dead to-night. . . . I remember when the old king died, the old king with the amber eyes and the gentle voice, that there was an old knight there who was in the old wars. He was so old that no one knew when he was born or who was his father. They said that he was born before the world began. . . . I think, perhaps, he was never born. . . .

MARIANE. Yes, I have heard of him, Pélissier. . . . It was Aggravette who told me, your cousin Aggravette. . . . We had been one day over the lake in a great galley. The rowers rowed. They rowed hard.

They were great men, and their muscles gleamed in the sun. . . .

*Enter* A MAN

THE MAN. X22, what are you doing off your beat ?

CURTAIN

modern, should sometimes forget she is a woman, but should always forget she is married. No, Dora, you are not married. [*Sighing.*] I sometimes wish you were.

HAROLD *and* ETHELRED. I think we must be going The worst of going is that it implies coming back. Good-bye.

[*They go out*

DORA. Did you really mean what you said . . . Cyril ?

CYRIL. Yes ; I really meant what I said.

DORA. So there's no more to be said.

[*They embrace*

CYRIL. The worst of engagements is that they seldom end in marriage. The worst of marriage is that it always begins with an engagement. Whenever I am engaged I always feel as though even marriage would be preferable. I have always felt that except when I have been married. Only last week I was married and I felt like it then. I married one of my housemaids. I felt that it was time I introduced economy into my household. I have always been as poor as a church mouse because I have had to maintain so many servants. Being a man with a stronger will-power than my friends suspect I came to a determined resolution. I made up my mind that I would diminish the number of my servants, and I could only do that by marrying them one by one and retaining their services without salary.

DORA. A wife in times saves nine.

CYRIL [*severely*]. I suspect, Dora, that that means nothing. Rolling stones always gather moss. I am not a rolling stone and I have gathered no moss.

[*Sadly.*] No, I fear the moss has gathered me. That is the worst of moss ; it is so avaricious. I am a prey to every grasping moss whose path I cross. There is old Moses Moss for example.

DORA. Oh, Cyril, you don't mean to say you have fallen into the hands of those horrid moneylenders ?

CYRIL. No, Dora ; would that it were so ; they might have lent me some money. As it is I have only been able to borrow from complete strangers. I do it at night with the help of a kindly policeman who was at college with me. He has risen in the world ; I have come down. I think he got his job through influence. That is the worst of influence ; it is so influential.

DORA. I am really awfully sorry for you, Cyril ; I would do anything for you except break our engagement.

CYRIL. No ; I do not ask you to do that, Dora. As a man makes his bed so he must lie, even if he makes it up a tree. That is the worst of trees ; they are so up. I think that trees should have grown horizontally ; they would have been more easy to descend. I once knew a man who had a mustard-tree. But the birds of the air did not build their nests in it [*sighing*], so he cut it down.

DORA. I think I hear father coming.

*Enter* MR. ASHINGTON

DORA. Father, Cyril and I are going to be married.

MR. ASHINGTON [*shaking hands with* CYRIL). My dear fellow, there's nothing could have delighted me more. A wife, as Solomon said, is better than rubies.

CYRIL. Who was Solomon ?

CURTAIN

# III

## SCHOOL OF REBELLION AND STAGE DIRECTIONS

## THE CAGED EAGLET

### OR, HOW WE MAKE OUR PLAYS READABLE

[*The scene is the morning-room at the Blenkinsops'. Chairs, books, pictures, etc. Sofa* R.C., *doors* R., R.C., L., *and* L.C. ; *French-window between centre doors if there is sufficient space.* MRS. BLENKINSOP *is seated at a large writing-desk against the right wall and her daughter* EUPHROSYNE *is writing at a smaller desk facing the opposite wall.* MRS. BLENKINSOP *is a lady past middle age, portly, treble-chinned, large-bosomed, hook-nosed, and pince-nez'd. She looks—as indeed she is—the type of prosperous philistinism. When* MR. BLENKINSOP *was first engaged to her she was a plump and stupid damsel in much request at tennis-parties. Years have aged and rounded her ; she does not play tennis nowadays ; in fact, her only exercise consists of taking her dog out for a daily drive in a victoria. She is engaged in writing a letter to a Mrs. Pott-Wither asking her whether she is willing to go halves in a garden-party on behalf of the local branch of the Degenerate Tinkers' Aid Society. It is not easy to guess how* EUPHROSYNE *has put up with her so long. At last, after several minutes busy scratching, she turns her head towards her daughter.*

MRS. BLENKINSOP. Euphrosyne !

[EUPHROSYNE *turns with an impatient look. She has for some time been secretly a member of the Syndicalist Party of Great Britain and Ireland. Her smooth hair, parted in the middle, her grey, direct eyes, and her square jaw, all betray resolution and originality. Only her strong sense of duty has kept her at home so long. She has no more sympathy with her asinine parents than you or I would have ; but she knows that in their way they are fond of their only child. Lately, however, domestic bonds have irked her more and more, and an explosion may be expected at any moment. She frowns slightly and bites her lower lip. Still, she answers.*

EUPHROSYNE. Yes, mother.

[MRS. BLENKINSOP *is blissfully unaware of her daughter s irritation, and she smiles fatly as she half-turns and surveys the neatly dressed figure. Probably she wonders as she looks at her whether or not she will marry Albert Pott-Wither, brother-in-law of Mrs. Pott-Wither, a bald-headed, nut-faced stockbroker of forty-five. But she puts such thoughts temporarily out of her head and resumes the conversation.*

MRS. BLENKINSOP. Do you remember the number of Mrs. Pott-Wither's house ?

[EUPHROSYNE *is naturally annoyed at the triviality of the interruption, but succeeds in stemming the tide of anger. Nevertheless her breast heaves rather quickly as she replies.*

EUPHROSYNE. Oh, I think it is 24 Hazelville Road, but I am not quite sure.

[*Both resume their writing, but after a couple of minutes* MRS. BLENKINSOP *looks up again, patting her hair lightly with her hand. She gives a little cough.*

MRS. BLENKINSOP. Do you know whether the Pott-Withers have changed their telephone number ?

EUPHROSYNE. No ; 664 Bracton.

MRS. BLENKINSOP. I thought it was 663.

EUPHROSYNE. No ; 664.

[*They continue writing until the elder woman rises to go to the telephone. She goes out door* R.C.. EUPHROSYNE *springs from her chair and begins kicking the ground. She paces hurriedly up stage and then returns to her chair.*

EUPHROSYNE. Oh, damn !

[MRS. BLENKINSOP *re-enters from the door by which she has emerged. She stands for a moment near the door scrutinising her daughter's bent back with a puzzled look. Then she gives a little sigh of non-comprehension and returns to her work. After a quarter of an hour's silence the door* R.C. *is suddenly flung open and* MR. BLENKINSOP *appears framed in the darkness behind it. He is very short, very stout, very shiny, very bald. His frock-coat flows back from an ample white-and-striped waistcoat whereon glitters a gold watch-chain with many seals. He wears spats. That is the kind of man he is. Once for a short time he sat on the local Board of Guardians ; but finding that there was very little to be made out of it, owing to the nature of his business, he retired after one term of service. Since then he has taken no part whatever in public life. He regards his daughter as a pretty young fool and sneers at her attempts to get in touch with modern movements. He hems loudly ; then slowly rolls up to the sofa, on which, with great care and effort, he deposits himself at full length.*

MR. BLENKINSOP. Well, Euphrosyne, haven't you got a word for me ?

[EUPHROSYNE *leaps up, her fist clenched, her cheeks aflame. She is looking splendid and knows it ; but after all, she can't help that. She remembers her childhood, but puts the thought out of mind. The climax has come.*

EUPHROSYNE. I won't. By God, I won't.

[*Her father quivering with rage looks at her lithe, erect form. He contemplates for a moment the notion of knocking her down and flogging her with his umbrella; on second thoughts he doubts his capacity for an enterprise so perilous. After all, he is not, he remembers, so young as he was.*

MR. BLENKINSOP. Come along ; none o' your nonsense.

[EUPHROSYNE *takes up an inkpot and brandishes it in a minatory manner. This is the last straw. As she begins her harangue she speaks in a low, tense, level voice ; but as she proceeds her voice rises until to her quailing parents it seems as though all the elements had been let loose.*

EUPHROSYNE. None of my nonsense. No ; you sha'n't have any more of my nonsense. Oh yes ; I've borne with you night and day, year after year, and I can tell you both I'm sick of it ; yes, sick of it. You wallowing beasts, you can think of nothing but eating and drinking. Do you think that I am cast in your own mould ? What right have you over me ? Yes, what right ? Year after year I have kept silence for your sakes. I have stifled and suffocated in the air of this house ; but now I am going away. Yes, I am going away. I am going away into the world. It is not food I want and rich clothes and dresses and flowers. I want life. You, you hogs, you do not know what life is. The sun does not shine for you, nor the winds blow, nor the mighty sea of heaven breathe its fragrance. You have never listened to the call of the moon and the chanting of the stars ; all the birds of the forest have sung in vain for you. But I want life. Yes, life. I have hungered and thirsted for life. I want to be free. I want to drink the clouds and take the planets to my arms. Faugh, you are no better than the beasts. You wake and sleep and to-morrow you die and perish utterly away. . . . By heaven, this is the end.

[*She picks up a large plant-pot and flings it through the French-window ; subsequently climbing through the hole she has made.* MRS. BLENKINSOP *sits at her desk weeping noisily into a large and vulgar handkerchief.* MR. BLENKINSOP *sits up dazed on his sofa. Now and then he whimpers like a hurt animal.*

MR. BLENKINSOP. Well. . . . Drat the little . . . . hussy.

CURTAIN

## IV

## MR. GILBERT MURRAY

## EURIPIDES UP-TO-DATE

[*Terrace of the palace at Mycenæ.* AGAPEMONE, *deserted by Noeus, paces distractedly up and down half-listening to the consoling words of her* NURSE. *The* CHORUS *of handmaidens are ranged at the back, washing their dirty linen in public.*

AGA. O light that blew from Colchis o'er the sea
Dost thou not dim and darken ? But for me
Blossoms a greater light, and all my breath
Pales ; and the dusty avenues of death
Call with a haven for fulfillèd feet
And violet grass and trees and waters sweet.
O in the untrodden pastures no man knows,
Cypris, thy hands have raised a lovelier rose
Than all of Argos or the Bactrian land
Ever man gathered.

NURSE. Daughter, stay thy hand,
Wag not the tongue of steel. 'Twère deadlier sin
To bare thy bird-bright throat and thrust therein,
Than hers of Pomphalos who, on a day,
Slew both her aged parents as men say
Cold as the mountains. . . .

AGA. Hold thy counsel, crone !
Far off from dark Cythera faintlier blown
A cry comes through the dawn that throbs the dawn
Swifter than goats' feet on the dewless lawn,
Death, death.

CHO. Who has encountered Death,
Death and the nets of Fate,
Who knows the step and the breath
The lintel and the gate ?
Lo ! even now have her eyes beholden
The ashes of love and the gateway golden
Foreseen long since in Argos olden
And the marble house long desecrate.

A cry from the great sea rings
Desolate, alien,
Of gods and ancient things
And war and the slaying of men ;
She hears the echo on roof and rafter
Of scorn and weeping and hollow laughter,
And tumults and storms and silence after
And feet that pass and come not again.

NURSE. Hear now the speech of these who see thy grief.

AGA. A broken petal and a transient leaf.

NURSE. Time has a potent salve for every smart.

AGA. Who has contrived a medicine for the heart ?

NURSE. Nathless our sires were wiser men than we.

AGA. Our dams, I hope, less garrulous . . . . Let be !

CHO. Who may withstand thee, Love, who may frustrate desire ?
Thy hands are the hands of Fate and thine eyes more fierce than fire,
Thy wings are plumed with mirth, with joy thy feet are shod,

But the darkling wind that bears thee blows from the throne of God.*

AGA. Mine eyes quiver and shake, my lips are mute.

NURSE. Rash queens ere now have gathered bitter fruit.

AGA. Nathless I think that you will shortly see
The very last of Agapemone.

NURSE. What folly's this ?

AGA. O but to tread once more
My father's halls and find again the Shore
Of Tenedos. Ah, there from dawn to dusk
In happy fields of amaranth and musk
My little sister Emmeline and I
Have, ah ! so often, chased the butterfly ;
White was the sunlight there, and bright the grass
Or ever between my maiden lips did pass
The bane of bitter bread. O could I roam
Thee, Tenedos, and the floors of the old home,
Thoughtless and free in the place where I was born. . . .
But see, with a piercing flame I am parched and torn,
This is the end ; O ye who now remain
Weep for a thing forsaken, a queen self-slain.

NURSE. What, wouldst thou slay thyself ? What, is this the end ?
Stay now thy hand, for Death's a treacherous friend!

AGA. I go, O halls of Tenedos, I go
Into the dark, the dark I do not know.

NURSE. What meanest thou thus gabbling of the dark ?

* Emendations ; as also *passim.*

Methinks thy statements overshoot the mark.

AGA. No wind blows always, ever one wind blows
Whither and why and wherefore no man knows*
And the Fates are blind and deaf and the gods are dumb
As woman's life. . . . See now, I come, I come.

[*Stabs herself*

NURSE. Woe! Woe! Whoever would have thought it,
Cursed be the deed and cursed be him who brought it.

CHO. I heard a sound by the city wall
As of children weeping and men sighing,
A sound of waters and stones that fall,
And maidens wounded and old men dying.
A mighty shouting and ululation
Of death, disaster and damnation.
For truth is hidden and knowledge vain,
And the gods indulge in frightful crimes,
As also, in fairness I add, do men.
And, to cut a long story short, till Time's
Vintage last-grown fulfils the cup
We never can tell what may turn up.

* Emendations; as also *passim.*

## V

## SOCIAL STUDY SCHOOL

### THE STRIFE OF THE BLATHERSKITES;

#### OR, THE STRONG-MINDED MANUFACTURER

[*The scene is the dining-room in Mr. Blatherskite's house. It is the fifty-third week of the strike. The chimneys of the works, which can be seen through the window, are smokeless. Occasionally there are borne on the wind through the open window the moans of starving people and the angry hoots of strikers who are listening to an incendiary speech by one of their leaders. Old* MR. BLATHERSKITE, *who, by a curious and convenient coincidence, has a face exactly like Mr. Norman M'Kinnell's, sits on a hard chair* L.C. *facing the audience. His lips are pursed grimly, his grey rock-like head is supported by a strong hand. He does not move, but meditates. There is two minutes' silence, which at last he breaks with a monosyllable.*

MR. BLATHERSKITE. Pah!

[*He is silent again. Enter from door* R. GERALD BLATHERSKITE. *his son, a fair-haired youth with a small diaphanous moustache. He hesitates as he watches his motionless sire, but at last plucks up courage to walk up to him though not to look him in the face.*

GERALD. Father!

MR. BLATHERSKITE. Well?

GERALD. Father. . . . Two hundred strikers' children have died of starvation since yesterday.

MR. BLATHERSKITE. Well ?

GERALD [*After uneasy hesitation*]. Oh, father, can't you do anything for them ?

MR. BLATHERSKITE. I am not responsible for them.

GERALD. Oh, for God's sake, father, give them some food.

MR. BLATHERSKITE. Let them return to work.

GERALD. They would, father, if you would meet them half-way.

MR. BLATHERSKITE. They have had my views on that subject.

GERALD. But if you don't they will all starve to death.

MR. BLATHERSKITE. Let them starve.

GERALD. But . . .

MR. BLATHERSKITE [*Picking up a newspaper and reading with an indifferent air*]. You may go.

[GERALD *walks a yard up stage ; then turns and looks at his father, makes as if to speak, thinks better of it, and silently goes out, shutting the door quietly behind him.*

MR. BLATHERSKITE. Pah !

[*Enter from door* L. HELEN BLATHERSKITE, *determined-looking and artily dressed. She means to take a firm stand, so begins by pulling over a chair to her father's vicinity and taking a firm seat.* MR. BLATHERSKITE *does not look up.*

HELEN. Father !

MR. BLATHERSKITE. Well ?

HELEN. This dispute has simply got to stop.

MR. BLATHERSKITE. The men can stop it when they like.

HELEN. You don't realise how awful the suffering in the village is.

MR. BLATHERSKITE. How the devil do you know what I realise?

HELEN. Oh, but you can't or you would agree to anything.

MR. BLATHERSKITE. You seem to be as great a fool as your mother and almost as great a fool as your brother. You may leave the roon.

HELEN [*standing up with crimson cheeks and quivering hands*]. I will not leave the room. You must hear me. Your barbarity is the talk of the county. If you resist much longer I am certain the men will murder us all.

MR. BLATHERSKITE. They are too cowardly for that.

[*He goes to the bell, rings it, and returns to his chair and his impassive attitude. Enter* PARLOURMAID.

MR. BLATHERSKITE. Wills, you may show Miss Helen out of the room.

[HELEN, *after a passionate gesture, leaves the room, the domestic following her.*

MR. BLATHERSKITE. Pah!

[*The domestic returns*

PARLOURMAID. There is a woman with a baby to see you, sir. She says her name is Parker.

MR. BLATHERSKITE. Bring her in.

[PARLOURMAID *goes out and returns with a pale, haggard woman in a ragged shawl, carrying a dirty bundle. The woman stands trembling, and then rushing forward flings herself on her knees in front of the manufacturer.*

MR. BLATHERSKITE [*Slightly raising his eyebrows but not turning his head*]. Well?

MRS. PARKER. Oo-oo-oo-oo-oo. Five of my babies are dead and this is the last.

MR. BLATHERSKITE. Interesting, but irrelevant.

MRS. PARKER. Oh, sir, my Jim was such a good husband. He has worked for you for twenty-five years, and he has never said a word against you, even since they came out on strike.

MR. BLATHERSKITE. He is on strike. He broke his agreement.

MRS. PARKER. Oh, sir, he didn't want to, sir. But he didn't want to be a blackleg.

MR. BLATHERSKITE. He can work if he comes back.

MRS. PARKER. Oh, sir, he can't come back until the others do. Not until you meet the leaders.

MR. BLATHERSKITE. Then he will not come back.

MRS. PARKER [*holding out infant*]. My baby is nearly dead, sir . . . it is my last one.

MR. BLATHERSKITE [*adjusting his pince-nez and cursorily examining the baby*]. Yes. So it appears.

[*He goes to the bell and rings it ; then returns to his seat and his attitude. Enter* PARLOURMAID.

MR. BLATHERSKITE. Show this woman to the door.

[*Exit* PARLOURMAID *and* MRS. PARKER, *sobbing hysterically*.

MR. BLATHERSKITE. Hum. Pah !

[*Enter* A STRIKER *through the window. Looking stealthily around him he sees the motionless figure. Believing it to be asleep he steals on tip-toe into the room and draws a knife*.

MR. BLATHERSKITE. I see you. You are a thief like the rest.

THE STRIKER [*dropping his knife in terror*]. I am not a thief. . . . I came to kill you.

MR. BLATHERSKITE [*still immobile*]. Ah! you came to kill me. Do you still feel like it? You had better come when I am asleep. It might require less courage then.

STRIKER [*passionately*]. You swine! You are not worth killing. . . . By God! it is you that are the murderer. My wife died last night.

MR. BLATHERSKITE. Ah! She was doubtless a fool like other women. You may go.

[THE STRIKER, *in trembling revulsion, retreats through the window, leaving his knife where it fell.* MR. BLATHERSKITE *rises, walks to it, picks it up, tries the edge along his thumb, and then flings it contemptuously into the waste-paper basket. He returns to his chair and lights a pipe.*

MR. BLATHERSKITE. Pah!

CURTAIN

## VI

## COTTAGE INTERIOR SCHOOL

## OUR VIVID RUSTICS

[*Interior of a cottage; door* R. *leading out, door* L. *leading upstairs, fireplace with log fire, oak settle, and coloured prints on the wall, including images of the King and Queen in their coronation robes. Table in middle, at which* ETHEL BOFFIN *stands peeling potatoes.*

ETHEL [*sings*].

O flaming poppies, cornflowers blue,
  Beyond the utmost hill,
The edge o' the world is fair to view
  And all the woods are still.

'Alf past vour and 'im not in yet. 'E was allus like that, late fer every mortal thing. I 'member when I was a-waitin' fer 'im at the altar, and me so fine and vitty in my magenter dress an' all, and him there a-turnin' up two hours late and passen a-cussin' 'im like a good 'un. Ah, deary me, deary me.

[*The door slowly opens and* ALGERNON TUPP, *the postman, cautiously peers in. Observing that she is alone he steps boldly over the threshold. His step startles her and she springs round.*

ETHEL. Oh, Algy, you did give me a turn like. I thought it was me 'usbink.

ALGY [*chuckling*]. He-he. Don't you wish as 'ow it was, eh? [*Coming nearer.*] 'Aven't you got a little kiss for I?

ETHEL [*pushing him away*]. Go on now, Mr Tupp, doan't 'ee be so silly now.

ALGY. Oo be you a-callin' silly ? If I keared I might say you was silly, too ; yes, and prove it too. An' what's more, there's more nor me knows it.

ETHEL [*clutching the table and gasping*]. What's that you'm a-sayin' of ?

ALGY [*getting bolder*]. You know very well what I'm a-sayin', an' 'is name begins with G., in my opinion.

ETHEL [*making a show of indifference*]. Well, you can keep your silly fancies to yourself. George Tibbits is wuth twenty of the likes of you, and if you say a word more about it I'll give yer somethink in the ear'ole wot you won't forgit.

ALGY. Eh wot ? That's 'ow it is, is it.

[*Sidles towards her to kiss her.*

ETHEL [*taking up the peeling-knife she has dropped*]. Take that, you swine !

[*Stabs him in the carotid artery ; he drops, bleeding freely and obviously dead. She looks around distractedly and, hearing a step at the door, hastily stows the body into the oven and stands over the spilt blood. Enter her husband,* TOM BOFFIN, *a hulking, drink-sodden fellow whose flabby features are the wreck of a once handsome face. He lurches forward with a dazed look.*

TOM [*hiccoughing*]. Oop. . . . . Got any beer, you . . . oop . . . little sow ?

ETHEL. Not for you, you drunken beast. You've 'ad beer and enough these five years. And me never 'ad a baby.

TOM [*striking her*]. 'Ere . . . oop . . . you get me some beer.

ETHEL [*stabbing him in the left breast*]. There's yer beer, you boozy 'og.

TOM *drops dead, and his wife drags him along by the hair and puts him into the left oven. Whilst she is in the act the door leading from the house opens and her* GRANDFATHER *comes in. He is abstracted, and notices nothing. He hobbles to the settle and with rheumatic groaning sits down on it.*

GRANFER. Well, Ethel, my vlower ? 'Specs Tom'll be in zoon. Ees, Tom'll be in zoon. Ees, Tom'll be in zoon. Ees, Tom'll be in zoon. Ees, Tom——

ETHEL [*impatiently interrupting him*]. Shut up, you ole warmint.

GRANFER [*whining*]. Ees, the childer is all like that in these days. She called me an ole warmint, she did. Ees, an ole warmint. Ees, an ole warmint. Ees, an ole warmint. Ees, an ole——

ETHEL [*springing at him with the knife*]. Gr-r-r-r.

[*Stabs him in the eye, the end of the knife protruding through the back of his head. The body falls to the ground and she leaves it there. The door opens and* GEORGE TIBBITS *appears. He looks at her with eager expectancy.*

GEORGE. Well, 'ave you bin an' done it ?

ETHEL [*triumphantly*]. Yes, I bin and done it. I done 'im in, an' I done granfer in an' I done Algy Tupp in. They was all fules every one of 'em. Two of 'em be in the oven and the other [*kicking* GRANFER *under the table*] is een 'ere.

GEORGE. All right, my angel of heaven. They'm a good ole damn good riddance, all on 'em. We'll put 'em all down the well, my pearl. 'Ave you got a kiss for I ?

ETHEL [*falling into his arms*]. 'Ave I ? [*Kisses him on both cheeks and then on the nape of the neck*]. Oh, George, I've dreamed of you night and day. In the corn fields I have let my hair down and bound it with fillets of poppies and garlands of cornflowers, and I have said " These are for my George, for the man with eyes like stars and a neck like a pillar of carven ivory." Oh, George, you don't know what it's been like waitin' all these years. I thought this time would never come. If I'd had a child I think I should have been able to stand it, a child who would have tugged at my hair with his pretty hands and called me mother. Oh, I've been so lonely . . . the stars . . . the night . . . the hills . . . the waves of the great sea.

[*Wanderingly singing.*

The edge o' the world is fair to view
And all the woods are still.

[*She faints in his arms.*

GEORGE. Yes, my sweeting, it has been a bit of a strain on you, I dare say. O my woman of all women, we will walk together, we two, in the sunlight and the moonlight, and all the past will fall away like a dark cloak.

ETHEL [*waking*]. Where am I ?

GEORGE [*patting her head*]. Here, my darling. Have you got any beer ?

CURTAIN.

# II

# HOW THEY DO IT

## No. 1. MR. H. BELLOC

### I

At Martinmas, when I was born,
*Hey diddle, Ho diddle, Do,*
There came a cow with a crumpled horn,
*Hey diddle, Ho diddle, Do.*
She stood agape and said, "My dear,
You're a very fine child for this time of year,
And I think you'll have a taste in beer,"
*Hey diddle, Ho diddle, Ho, do, do, do,*
*Hey diddle, Ho diddle, Do.*

A taste in beer I've certainly got,
*Hey diddle, Ho diddle, Do,*
A very fine taste that the Jews have not,
*Hey diddle, Ho diddle, Do.*
And though I travel on the hills of Spain,
And Val-Pont-Côte and Belle Fontaine,
With lusty lungs I shall still maintain
*Hey diddle, Ho diddle, Ho, do, do, do,*
*Hey diddle, Ho diddle, Do.*

So Sussex men, wherever you be,
*Hey diddle, Ho diddle, Do,*
I pray you sing this song with me,
*Hey diddle, Ho diddle, Do*;
That of all the shires she is the queen,
And they sell at the "Chequers" at Chancton-
bury Green

The very best beer that ever was seen.
*Hey Dominus, Domine, Dominum, Domini, Domino,*
*Domino.*

## II

Lord Globule was a backward lad,
Round leaden eyes Lord Globule had,
And shambling legs and shoulders stooped,
And lower lip that dripped and drooped.
At ten years old he could not get
The hang of half the alphabet ;
At twelve he learnt to read his name,
At seventeen to write the same,
At twenty-one, his boyhood done,
He reached the age of twenty-one,
Which was sufficient reason why
His father's sturdy tenantry
Should gather in a large white tent,
Engulf some tons of nutriment,
And, freely primed with free potations,
Emit profuse congratulations.

Sweet twenty-one ! O magic age !
The opulent youth surveys the stage
Where soon he'll walk 'mid loud applause.
He only hesitates because
His family all have different views
Which rôle, which entrance he should choose.
Lord Globule's father thought him made
To dominate the world of Trade ;
" Finance, finance is more his line,"
Exclaimed his Uncle Rubinstein ;
" Oh, no," Aunt Araminta cried,

## HOW THEY DO IT

" Diplomacy should first be tried " ;
But in the end with one accord
They thought the chances of a hoard
That British politics afford
Would suit Lord Globule's pocket best.

They all employed their interest
With Uncle Tom, and Moses Kant,
And Strauss, who married Globule's aunt,
And Johnny Burke, and Stoke and Shere,
And the old Duke and Humphrey Bere ;
So that in January next year
A vacancy in Hertfordshire
Offered itself, and Globule's parts
Enraptured the electors' hearts.

The next five Sessions saw him slip
Through Private Secretaryship,
Under-Secretaryship,
Financial Secretaryship,
To Secretaryship of State,
With absolute power to regulate
The rural and the urban rate
Of birth among the pauper classes,
His duty 'twas to scan the masses
And carefully eliminate
What seemed to him degenerate,
To say what kinds they'd mutilate
And which ones merely isolate
In " homes from home " where they should be
Looked after tender-heartedly
By men selected by a Board
(No fewer than twenty to each ward).

A heavy task, as you'll agree,
For which they paid him liberally.
Globule the office still would grace,
And still would draw the emolument,
Had not a wretched accident
Unfortunately taken place.

His chief subordinate being away
(The man who wrote Lord Globule's speeches),
Lord Globule took a holiday,
Going by train to Burnham Beeches,
A secretary, tall and prim,
As usual, escorting him.
This tall young gentleman, when taxed
Later, denied he had relaxed
His customary watchfulness ;
But be that as it may, 'tis certain
That late that night at Shoeburyness
Lord Globule was discovered bare
Of all except a muslin curtain
And some few feathers in his hair
And that the constable, when he
Was quite unable to explain
His actions or identity,
Concluded that he was insane.
Next day before the magistrate
The poor young pillar of the State
(His curtain bore no laundry marks !)
Was still quite unidentified,
And, catechized once more, replied
Only with sundry mews and barks.
And ultimately (to cut short
The day's proceedings in the court)

## HOW THEY DO IT

Two doctors and the police advised
That Globule should be sterilized
(A thing I need not further mention),
And sent to permanent detention.

For days the public did not hear
Of Globule's disappearance ; near
And far, inquiries set on foot
Quite privately, produced no fruit,
Until at last the rumour spread
(Not in the papers) and some one said
That such a man in such a dress
Had been detained at Shoeburyness.
His relatives pursued the clue ;
Alas, alas, the thing was true,
'Twas poor young Globule . . .
But the worst
Was this : that when they'd brought him out
They found the thing had got about
Among the unenlightened mob,
Which stultified beyond all doubt
The hopes they'd entertained at first
That Globule might preserve his job.
Fate was too strong ; they had to bow ;
Globule at home had been a failure ;
And they could only give him now
The Governorship of South Australia.

## No. 2. MR. W. H. DAVIES

### I

I'm sure that you would never guess
  The tales I hear from birds and flowers,
Without them sure 'twould be a mess
  I'd make of all the summer hours;
But these fair things they make for me
A lovely life of joy and glee.

I saw some sheep upon some grass,
  The sheep were fat, the grass was green,
The sheep were white as clouds that pass,
  And greener grass was never seen;
I thought, "Oh, how my bliss is deep,
With such green grass and such fat sheep!"

And as I watch bees in a hive,
  Or gentle cows that rub 'gainst trees,
I do not envy men who live,
  No fields, no books upon their knees.
I'd rather lie beneath small stars
Than with rough men who drink in bars.

## HOW THEY DO IT

### II

A poor old man
  Who has no bread,
He nothing can
  To get a bed.

He has a cough,
  Bad boots he has ;
He takes them off
  Upon the grass.

He does not eat
  In cosy inns
But keeps his meat
  In salmon tins.

No oven hot,
  No frying-pan ;
Thank God I'm not
  That poor old man.

## No. 3. SIR HENRY NEWBOLT

It was eight bells in the forenoon and hammocks running sleek
(*It's a fair sea flowing from the West*),
When the little Commodore came a-sailing up the Creek
(*Heave Ho ! I think you'll know the rest*),
Thunder in the halyards and horses leaping high,
Blake and Drake and Nelson are listenin' where they lie,
Four and twenty blackbirds a-bakin' in a pie,
And the *Pegasus* came waltzing from the West.

Now the little Commodore sat steady on his keel
(*It's a fair sea flowing from the West*),
A heart as stout as concrete reinforced with steel
(*Heave Ho ! I think you'll know the rest*).
Swinging are the scuppers, hark, the rudder snores,
Plugging at the Frenchmen, downing 'em by scores.
Porto Rico, Vera Cruz, and also the Azores,
And the *Pegasus* came waltzing from the West.

So three cheers more for the little Commodore
(*It's a fair sea flowing from the West*).
I tell you so again as I've told you so before
(*Heigh Ho ! I think you know the rest*).
Aged is the Motherland, old but she is young
(Easy with the tackle there—don't release the bung),
And I sang a song like all the songs that I have ever sung
When the *Pegasus* came sailing from the West.

## No. 4. MR. JOHN MASEFIELD

### I. THE POET IN THE BACK STREETS

[Author's Note.—The following poem has been considerably compressed owing to the exigencies of space, which must sometimes be respected.

I

Down Lupus Street there is a little pub,
  And there there worked a little bright-haired
      maiden,
Mornings the furniture she had to scrub,
  Evenings she'd walk about with pewters laden ;
  But still she sang as did the birds in Eden ;
In fact you would have said that there was no
More cheerful barmaid in all Pimlico.

She had eleven brothers and a sister,
  A mother who had rheumatism bad,
And when she left o' mornings how they missed her,
  And when she stayed o' Sundays weren't they
      glad ;
  No other help or maintenance they had,
So that their mother often said, " God pink 'em,
Lucky for them Flo makes a decent income.

" If 'twasn't for Flo's fifteen bob a week,
Me and them brats would not know where to turn,
For some of 'em ain't old enough to speak,
And none of 'em ain't old enough to earn,
And as for 'er bright merry japes, why, durn
My bleedin' eyes, if we'd no Flo to quirk us,
I'm sure we'd soon be droopin' in the workus.

" It's only Flo's 'igh spirits keeps me goin'
The way she sings ' My Pansy,' it's a treat,
And also ' All a-blowin' and a-growin',
Our Flo is fair top-'ole, she can't be beat.
So give three cheers for Flo, its' time to eat ;
Mary, you just run out and fetch some jam,
And Bill, take down the pickles and the ham."

So the years passed, so Florence earned the money,
And all the throng were happy as could be,
No air could blench or stain her cheeks so bonny,
No labour weigh upon her heart so free,
She was, in short, as chirpy as could be ;
Until at last came Fate in Fate's own time,
And ravelled her in the dark nets of crime.

Crime is the foulest blot on our escutcheon,
Crime draws mankind as the moon draws the tides,
Crime is a thing I'm rather prone to touch on,
Crime is a clanking chain that grins and grides,
A lure, a snare, and other things besides ;
If crime should cease, I should not then be able
To furnish England with my monthly fa ble.

## HOW THEY DO IT

One foggy night it happened there were drinking,
Within the bar a crowd of all the boys,
'Erb Gupps and Nixey Snell and Snouty Jinkin,
And Noakes with several friends from Theydon Bois
Visiting Pimlico ; they made a noise
With call for booze and anecdote and curse,
And as the night wore on the row got worse.

" Wot sher," " Wot ho," " I don't fink," " Blast yer eyes,"
" That was a good 'un," " Cheese it," " 'Arf a mo,"
" Ten pints of 'arf an' 'arf," " There ain't no flies
On Nixey," " You're a —— welsher, Joe,"
" A quartern more, miss," " —— lie," and so
They kept it up with rapid thrust and answer,
In phrases neatly measured for a stanza.

Even when they yelled and fought, Flo did not mind,
She did not mind, for she was used to this,
Even when to sottish amourousness inclined
They called her " Floss," or " Flo," instead of " Miss " ;
But when at last drunk Snouty snatched a kiss,
She felt her cheek flame with a flaming flame,
She felt her heart scorch with a hell of shame.

All the air howls when storms scourge the Atlantic,
All the wide forest shakes when falls the boar,
A wounded whale is often very frantic,
And jealous lions have been known to roar

Almost as loud as breakers on the shore ;
But all these are tranquility and rest
Compared with what went on in Florrie's breast.

Red in her soul shame set its blazing seal,
Black in her heart strong hate swirled round in torrents,
Blue in her eyes the lightning shone like steel,
White on her lips rage mingled with abhorrence ;
Against a barrel's back leaned Barmaid Florence,
Watching with grinding teeth and eyeballs rolling,
Drunk Snouty who was belching forth "Tom Bowling."

There while the boozers rocked in song obscene,
She stood like a tall statue marble-still,
And first she moaned, " I am smirched, I am no more clean,"
And then she rasped, " By God, but I will kill
That lousy stinkard, yes, by God I will."
Fate flung the dice of Doom, her buckler buckled ;
Life shrank, grew pale ; Death rubbed his chin and chuckled.

So it draws on to closing-time ; men go
By twos and threes ; Flo washes pots and glasses,
Ranging them on the shelves in their degrees,
Wipes the wet counter dry, turns down the gasses ;
And, locking up the doors, the portal passes,
Grasping with fervour of a frenzied bigot
Inside her muff a mallet and a spigot.

There Snouty was, fumbling his way along
  Towards the bridge, blind-tight, alone and grunting,
And as he lurched he sang a maudlin song,
  A foolish song beginning, " Baby Bunting,
  For rabbit-skins your father's gone a-hunting,"
And as Flo heard the melody undroughty,
She whispered, " Cripes, *I'll* bunt you, Mr. Snouty ! "

So they went on, he foremost, she behind,
  Until they got to the Embankment wall ;
He leant against it ; swifter than the wind
  She smashed her wedge into his head, and all
  His brains spattered the stones in pieces small.
" My kiss," she hissed ; then with a sudden shiver
Fled, tipping tools and Snouty in the river.

And like a fleet slim panther she did fly
  Through the webbed streets of silent Pimlico,
Faithful the white stars glimmered in the sky,
  Over the Lambeth bank the moon hung low,
  A great round golden moon as white as snow.
Death cursed ; Life smiled and murmured, " She will live,
The police will fail to track the fugitive."

And the high stars looked down and saw her enter
  The doorway of her home in the dark street,
Happy to think the cops would never scent her,
  Proud for the godlike swiftness of her feet.
  Cheek to her pillow cried she : " Yes, 'twas sweet."

But God behind God's curtain cogitated
About another end, and all things waited.

II

Six months rolled by ; Flo earned her wonted wages,
  The family consumed its usual food.
Had nothing changed I'd not have penned these
    pages ;
  But evil generally brings forth good ;
  Briefly I'd have it to be understood
One day a pavement-preacher's casual sentence
Hurled Flo into abysses of repentance.

So the sky fell ; there came a hand of fire
  That seared her soul with consciousness of sin,
Her soul was all one yearning of desire
  For God ; she felt like jumping from her skin ;
  Like Hell in a through-draught she burnt within.
" Mother," she said, " here is my this week's sub.,
I cannot go on working at the pub."

The mother swooned ; the children joined in prayer
  That Flo should not decide in such a fast time ;
But the fierce heavens cried beer was a snare
  And skittles was a most immoral pastime ;
  So that that evening for the very last time
She washed the pots and locked the " Fountain "
    door,
As she had done so many nights before.

Next day she went out early without warning,
  Down the wan street ; and later in the day,

That is to say well on into the morning,
  She sent a District Messenger to say
  That she had definitely gone away
To join the Battersea Salvation Army.
" Swipe me," her mother moaned, " the gal's gone
    barmy."

Barmy or not, she certainly had gone,
  In her low attic poor old mother wept,
" She kep the home up, little Florence done,
  We was so happy in the home she kept ;
  'Twas mean of her to hook it while we slept ;
I'll larn her yet to take me by surprise,
I'll do her in, —— 'er —— eyes ! "

But Flo was meanwhile getting fur and furder.
  Safe in the barracks in the Bilsey Road,
Aching to make atonement for her murder,
  She said she wished to take up her abode
  There permanently ; stabbed by her inner goad,
She very quickly rose to the direction
Of her new comrades' Social Effort Section.

She visited the mothers in the slums,
  And daily rescued suicidal wretches,
She helped the young with their addition sums,
  And washed the infants' clothes and mended
    breeches ;
  And when she broke a plate or dropped some
    stitches,
None ever heard a hasty word from Flo,
The most she ever said was, " Here's a go ! '

Work or no work, her heart was always merry,
  Heaven had washed her heart and cleansed her
    eyes,
Adjutant Flo, the Barmaid Missionary,
  Was the adored of every sex and size,
  They said that she had strayed from Paradise,
And every week her saintly reputation
  Led many sinning souls to seek salvation.

Death laughed ; Life winced ; for in the neigh-
    bouring borough
  Old mother dwelt and bided her own hour,
Whetting a carving-knife with motions thorough,
  Practising stabs of accuracy and power.
  The scythe must fall, and then must fall the flower,
The day must die and then must sink the sun,
And all things end that ever have begun.

III

All the crowds crowd in Battersea's Green Park ;
  The deer are fed, the ducks quack on the water ;
On the trim paths the Sabbath-resting clerk
  Walks slowly with his wife and son and daughter,
  Or seeks the grass where orators breathe slaugh-
    ter,
Some singing hymns to variegate their turns,
Or waving flags with portraits of John Burns.

Middle the plot there brays a brazen band,
  Peaked caps, red jerseys, other things of blue ;
And when they cease behold a figure stand,

A bright-haired wench who wears those garments
too.
She preaches truth as few but she can do
Concerning drink and cigarettes and betting
So that the mob must listen though they're sweat-
ing.

" S'welp me, it's hot." " Yes, s'welp me, so it is."
" Ain't it a shame the pubs ain't open Sundays,
Just as they be Tuesdays and Wednesdays, Liz,
Thursdays, Fridays, Saturdays, and Mondays,
To close the —— up on just this one day's
'Bout the worst thing the —— law has done."
" Yus, so it is." " Gorblimey, wot a sun ! "

But though the high sun spilled a raging heat,
They could not go, they had to stay and hear,
So tense her accents were, her voice so sweet.
" Crikey," says Bill, " she's a 'ard egg, no fear."
Says Sam, " by Gosh, I'll drop the —— beer."
" You won't." " I will." " You won't." " What
will you bet ? "
" A . . . no, by gum, 'ere comes a Suffragette ! "

It was a Suffragette with purple banner,
Handbell and bag of many-coloured bills,
At once in her inimitable manner
She draws the crowd ; the space around her fills,
While Flo's grows empty ; soon her pitch is still's
The solitudes of the Antarctic Ocean,
For even the band had shared the crowd's emotion.

Not a man trod her corner of the Park,
  A quarter-mile around the place was void,
Only her voice to one lost mongrel's bark
  Rang on, and still, as with sound texts she toyed,
  She did not seem the slightest bit annoyed.
But Life shrank low, and greedy Death did dance,
For here at last had come old mother's chance !

Old mother had been hiding 'hind a tree,
  Old mother who had sworn the end of Flo,
Weapon in hand she stole up stealthily
  Towards the daughter who had grieved her so.
  " Aha ! " she cried, " you little bitch, Ho, ho,
I'll pay you out now for your vile desertion . . . "
In Flo's plain blouse she made a neat insertion !

Flo fell, she fell, did Barmaid Flo, she fell ;
  The carving-knife was sticking in her back,
And as she fell she cried out, " Well, well, well,
  What is the motive of this base attack ? "
  But her old mother shrieked aloud, " Alack,
This was my child, this was my little child,
O, I must cover her with blossoms wild."

So sought she underneath the elms and oaks,
  Garlic and dandelions, peonies
And cabbage-wort and sprole and old-man's-mokes,
  And lillikens and dinks and bitter-ease,
  And mortmains that the hind in autumn sees
In places where the mist lies on the hay
And all the land is frozen with the May.

And with her arms full, poor old mother staggered
  To her poor child there dead upon the grass,
" My little Flo," she whimpered, " I'll be jaggered,
  I don't know how it ever come to pass,
  I don't know how I done it, little lass ;
Whyever did I sharp that carvin' knife
And let out all my lovely darlin's life ?

" She wor a merry grig, wor little Flo,
  She kep the family goin' nicely, she did,
There never was a wheeze she didn't know,
  She always pinched us anything we needed ;
  Cripes, but I cannot tell why I proceeded,
Just 'cos she left the family to starve,
My pretty Flo's sweet darlin' back to carve."

And so she brought the flowers to her dead,
  And piled them on her feet and face and breast,
Flo lay there still as down the blossoms shed,
  A heavenly angel lying down to rest,
  A downy bird at evening on its nest,
A cloud, a moth, a wave, a steamer, or
Almost any other metaphor.

" Good-bye, my little Flo," said poor old mother
  " You had your faults, I willingly admit,
Yet I am, taking one thing with another,
  Sorry for my rash act more than a bit,
  But still, I do not want to swing for it.
Mum is the word, least said is soonest mended."
So mother left the Park, and all was ended.

## II THE MERCIFUL WIDOW

Inside a cottage by a common
There lived an aged widow woman
She had twelve children (quite a lot),
And often wished that she had not.
" S'welp me," she often sighed, " I'd rather
You'd had a less prolific father ;
Better than raise this surging mob
That God had bowled me for a blob."

Amongst her seven strapping sons
There were some interesting ones.
Even the baby James, for instance,
Had killed a man without assistance ;
And several more in divers ways
Had striven to sing their Maker's praise.
Henry, quite small, had tried to smother
His somnolent recumbent mother ;
Which failing, when she hollered fearful,
He looked upon her quite untearful,
With something of Don Juan's calm,
Proceeding thus without a qualm :—
" O mother in our hours of ease,
As irritating as ten fleas,
When pain and anguish wring the brow
A fatuously lethargic sow,
This time I haven't put you through it,
But if you wait a day or two, it
Will be quite clear I mean to do it."
Whereat the mother murmured " Law !
I'll gi'e yer a wipe acrost the jaw ! "

Another son, Ezekiel,
Was well upon the road to hell,
Once every fortnight he betrayed
An unsuspecting village maid,
And now and then he went much furder
By rounding off the job with murder.
Sometimes they took him to the 'sizes,
But there he told outrageous lieses,
His loving family, unblushing,
Always unanimously rushing
To help him with false alibises.
Richard was just another such,
But William, Sam and John were much
More evil and debauched than these.
The account of their atrocities
Might make a smelting furnace freeze.
Without a scintilla of shame
They bragged of things I cannot name.
I represent them here by blanks.
— — — — — — — — — —
(READER : " For this relief much thanks ! ")

Hedda Lucrezia Esther Waters,
The eldest of the widow's daughters,
In early infancy absorbèd
A dreadful liking for the morbid.
She much preferred the works of Ibsen
To those of Mr. Dana Gibson,
And when she went to bed at night
She prayed by yellow candle-light :
" Six angels for my bed,
Three at foot and three at head,
Beardsley, Strauss, Augustus John,

Bless the bed that I lie on.
Nietzsche, Maeterlinck, Matisse,
Fold my sleep in holy peace."
The vices to which she inclined
Were peccadilloes of the mind.
Her sisters were much less refined,
And often when they sallied out,
With knife and pistol, kriss and knout,
And other weapons of the sort
Adapted to bucolic sport
And rural raptures in the dark,
They took occasion to remark :
" Why, wot the 'ell's the —— use
O' 'Edda, she ain't got no juice,
She'll gas and jabber till all's blue
She'll talk but she will never do.
Upon my oath, it is fair sickenin'."

And so at last they gave her strychnine,
A thing efficient though not gory.
And Hedda drops from out the story.

Four daughters, seven sons were left,
But still the widow felt bereft,
She was distressed at Hedda's loss,
And found it hard to bear her cross.
She tried to find a salve for it
By studying in Holy Writ.
She read the exciting episode
Of how good Moses made a road
Across the rubicundish ocean,
But could not stifle her emotion.
She read of Jews and Jebusites,

And Hittites and Amakelites,
And Joash, Job and Jeroboam,
And Rachel, Ruth and Rehoboam,
And Moloch, Moab and Megiddo,
But still no respite had the widow.
Nothing could charm her grief away,
It grew more bitter every day.
Often she'd sit when evening fell,
And moan : " Ah, Lawkamussy, well,
'Edda was better than the rest,
My 'Edda allus was the best.
Many's the time she's washed the crocks,
And scrubbed the floors and darned the socks.
When all them selfish gals an' blokes
Was out, the selfish things they are,
A-murderin' and a-rapin' folks,
'Edda would stay 'ome with 'er ma.
Yes, 'Edda was a lovely chile,
I do remember 'er sweet smile,
'Er little 'ands wot lammed and lugged me,
An' scratched an' tore an' pinched an' tugged me.
I mind me 'ow so long ago,
I set 'er little cheeks aglow,
When I 'ad bin to Ledbury fair
An' bought a ribbon for 'er 'air,
A ribbon for 'er pretty 'ead ;
But now my little 'Edda's dead !
Now while spring pulses through the blood
And jonquils carpet every wood,
And God's small fowls sing in the dawn,
I wish to Gawd I'd naver bin born ! "

And so at last the widow thought
Things were not going as they ought.
She'd never grumbled in the past :
She'd let them all do things at which
Most parents would have stood aghast—
She'd seen it all without a twitch.
Indeed, religiously she'd tried
To share the joy and fun they'd had ;
But really, this sororicide
Was coming it a bit too bad.
She made her mind up : " It's high time
They stopped their silly vice and crime ! "

She mustered the domestic throng
And gave it to them hot and strong.
" Look here," she said, " this —— flux
'Ad best come to a —— crux !
I long regarded as diversions
Your profligacies and perversions ;
I helped you while you swam in sin,
And backed you up through thick and thin ;
But now you've gone a step too far ;
I mean to show you I'm your ma.
Yes, it's you I'm talkin' to, Kate and John :
You'll have to stop these goings-on.
Murders must stop from this day on ! "

Sons and daughters stood amazed,
Bunkered, flummuxed, moonstruck, dazed,
Grunted with appropriate swear,
" What's come over the old mare ? "
" Stop the murders, stop the drink,
Stop the lechery ? I don't fink ! "

## HOW THEY DO IT

" If she's had enough of sin,
I guess we'd better do 'er in ! "
Thus said Henry, savagely
Whetting his knife upon his knee.
" No," said James, " go easy, brother ;
After all, she is our mother.
Just you wait for 'arf a mo'—
Give me 'arf a mo' to show
'Er the thing in a new light,
And mother'll come round all right ! "

Love is and was our king and lord,
The tongue is mightier than the sword,
Words may shine at break of day
Like a palace of Cathay,
Words may shine when evening falls
Like the sign of three brass balls.
All the crowd cried, " Righto, Jim !
Jim's a plucked 'un, 'ark to 'im ! "
Chewing half-a-pound of twist,
Smiting the table with his fist,
Jim went on : " Just 'ark to me,
Mother, jest you 'ark to me,"
(He spat with vigour on his hands)
" This is 'ow the matter stands.

" I'll agree we've done enough
Stabbin's, drunks and such-like stuff,
We, unlike our fellow-men,
Have fractured the commandments ten
With others of our own invention
That the scripture doesn't mention.
We have done to heart's content.

— — — — — — — — — —
— — — — — — — — — —

And speaking for myself, I've had
Quite enough of being bad ;
And to cut the matter short,
Should find uprightness quite good sport.
But, mother, mother, strike me blind,
This must aye be borne in mind,
Mother, mother, strike me rotten,
This must never be forgotten,
We must not think of self alone.
If no one's interests but our own
Were here involved we'd all turn pi,
And put our past transgressions by.
We'd gladly cease our evil-doings,
Promiscuous assaults and wooings,
And end the too-familiar scenes
Which you indignantly have eyed ;
Only, alas, our hands are tied,
Another factor intervenes.
For there's a poet up in London
Who, if we stop, will be quite undone,
We do evil for his good,
He inks his paper with our blood ;
Every crime that we commit
He makes a poem out of it,
And were we so unkind's to stop, he
Would famish for congenial copy.
My life begins to give my guts hell,
But there's the matter in a nutshell."

" Ay, ay," said Dick, in accents cold,
" Brother Jim the truth has told."

" Ay, ay," the girls said, " do not doubt it,
That's the truth, that's all about it."
" Well," said the mother, " I am human,
Though only a poor widow woman.
Jim's remarks have cleared my sight,
I understand your motives quite,
And when you shed pore 'Edda's blood
Your purpose was distinctly good.
I still must make it understood
I do not like your goings-on,
Espeshly yours, Bill, Sam and John.
But contraventions of the laws
Committed in such worthy cause,
Habits, however atavistic
Prompted by feelings altruistic,
I can't view with disapprobation
Entirely without qualification.
Thought of your evil deeds must pain me,
Thoughts of your motives must restrain me,
I'm proud to find such virtue in you,
As far as I'm concerned, continue."

## No. 5. MR. G. K. CHESTERTON

### I

When I leapt over Tower Bridge
There were three that watched below,
A bald man and a hairy man,
And a man like Ikey Mo.

When I leapt over London Bridge
They quailed to see my tears,
As terrible as a shaken sword
And many shining spears.

But when I leapt over Blackfriars
The pigeons on St. Paul's
Grew ghastly white as they saw the sight
Like an awful sun that falls ;

And all along from Ludgate
To the wonder of Charing Cross,
The devil flew through a host of hearts—
A messenger of loss.

With a rumour of ghostly things that pass
With a thunderous pennon of pain,
To a land where the sky is as red as the grass
And the sun as green as the rain.

## HOW THEY DO IT

### II

It is a curious thing about most modern people—it is possible that the ancients sometimes exhibited the same trait—that they will insist on making confusions. Sometimes they even make confusions worse confounded, but that particular species of the genus need not now detain us. More curious still—as Alice should have said but did not—their habit is not to confuse similar things but dissimilar things. They do not confuse Miss Marie Corelli with Mr. Hall Caine; they do not confuse six of one with half-a-dozen of the other; they do not even commit the very pardonable error of failing to distinguish between Mr. Asquith and Mr. Balfour. The case, indeed, is quite the reverse. They have a strange and almost horrible, a magical and most tragical power of differentiating at a glance between things that to the ordinary human eye would seem to be identical in every feature. They can draw a confident line between the Hegelians and the Pragmatists (of whom I am not one); they can call the Primitive Methodists, the Swedenborgians and the Socialists by their names; confront them with a flock of sheep and you will find them as expert ovine onomatologists as any wild and wonderful shepherd who ever brooded in the sunsets on the remote and inacessible hills of Dartmoor. But put before them two or three things that are really and fundamentally different, and they will be almost pitifully at a loss to detect the slightest diversity. They will know one octopus from another, but they will not know either from a lobster. They will know the average Tory from the average Socialist, but they will not know one kind of Socialist from another kind of Socialist.

This profound and far-reaching truth has frequently struck me ; and, as you doubtless know, I have as frequently expressed it. Our ancestors (who were much less foolish than some of their descendants) never hit the nail on the head with more stupendous and earth-shaking force than when they laid it down as a rigid and unquestionable axiom that the truth cannot be too often restated. It is that inexpugnable fact that plunges our modern pessimists into the nethermost abysses of suicidal despair ; it is that saline and saltating fact that raises in the breasts of our optimists a fierce and holy joy. The essence of a great truth is that it is stale. Sometimes it is merely musty, sometimes it is almost terribly mouldy. But mouldiness is not merely a sign of vitality—which is truncated immortality ; it is the sole and single, the one and only sign of vitality. Truth has gathered the wrinkles of age on her brows and the dust of ages on the skirts of her garment. A thing can no more be true and fresh than it can be new and mouldy. If a man told me he had discovered a new truth I should politely but firmly reprimand him precisely as I should a man who informed me, with however candid and engaging an air, that he had just seen moss growing on the back of a new-born child.

Meditating thus, I was walking last Tuesday night down the splendid and awful solitudes of the Old Kent Road. Diabolic shapes grinned and moved in the secret and sorrowful shadows of the shop doorways, and every looming warehouse seemed a monstrous sibyl writhing gnarled and boding fingers at the hurrying clouds. Suddenly as I turned a corner I saw, low in the sky where the houses were broken, a solitary star, a huge red star glowing and flickering with all the flames of hell, a star that in a more religious and less purblind age men would have whispered to be prophetic of awful and convulsive things. It held my feet as with gyves of iron. I gazed at its scarlet lamp, quaking and shivering like a man in a palsy. And then, full in my back, I felt a strange and horrible blow, and there rang in my ears a voice sepulchral and thunderously muffled as the voice of one come from the dead.

There were words, human articulate words, and they were addressed to me. There is something peculiarly mystic and terrible about words that proceed from an unknown mouth through impenetrable darkness. It is that, I think, that must have been the first principle grasped by the hairy and horrible men of the primeval forests. They went to some cave for a refuge and found a religion. They went there for a gorge and found a god. They went there for a repast and found a ritual. They entered the cave expecting to have a snooze, and when they left it they found they had a sacerdotalism. As I heard the loathsome voice hailing me through the darkness as some evil minion of Beelzebub might hail a lost and errant soul through the pierceless and intangible grottoes of the outer void, it suddenly, I say, flashed across my consciousness that the impalpable stranger was addressing me in articulate, not to say terse, syllables of the English tongue. If there is one thing more than another that accounts for the widespread use of the English language it is its incomparable and almost murderous terseness. A man once told me that Bulgarian was still more terse ; another man (presuming, I fear, on an old friendship) assured me a few months later that Bantu was terser than either ; but as Bulgarian and Bantu are studies of my youth that I have long left behind me, I am afraid I am not quite competent to express a final opinion on the matter. Suffice it that you would no more attempt to increase the terseness of the English tongue than you would attempt to augment the flexibility of an elephant's trunk by the insertion of an arrangement, however delicate and dexterous, of cogwheels.

His words were terse, but at first I did not altogether fathom their meaning. " How," I pondered, " surely there can be nothing sanguinary about me. I have not shaved myself for days, and I have not to my knowledge committed a murder for at least three weeks. And if there is anything markedly mural about my eyes I confess I was unaware of the fact. Indeed, it is not altogether plain to me how any eye can be mural. My friend, you must be mistaken."

Summoning up the courage that is often a strong characteristic of really brave men, I spoke to him. There was, in that dreadful and desolate place, under the fiery blaze of that lurid and lecherous planet, something hollow and awful even about the tones of my own voice. It echoed along the walls and wailed round the corners like the foggy clarion of a marshland ghost. But my heart was set like steel, and unquailing I cried, " I think, my friend, you have made a mistake."

And an error that was a type and a symbol became also a text.

. . . . . . .

When I had spoken he fled. Which showed that he was neither a man nor a democrat, but a puny and pessimistic modern—in all probability a Nietzschean. Under the sky, now cloudless and sprinkled with silver stars, I pursued my way, watching for the banners of the dawn, and listening for her trumpets that knew the youth of the world.

## No. 6. NUMEROUS CELTS

There's a grey wind wails on the clover,
  And grey hills, and mist around the hills,
And a far voice sighing a song that is over,
  And my grey heart that a strange longing fills.

A sheen of dead swords that shake upon the wind,
  And a harp that sleeps though the wind is blowing
Over the hills and the seas and the great hills behind,
  The great hills of Kerry, where my heart would be going.

For I would be in Kerry now where quiet is the grass,
  And the birds are crying in the low light,
And over the stone hedges the shadows pass,
  And a fiddle weeps at the shadow of the night.

With Pat Doogan
Father Murphy
Brown maidens
King Cuchullain
The Kine
The Sheep
Some old women
Some old men
And Uncle White Sea-gull and all.

(*Chorus*) And Uncle White Sea-gull and all.

## No. 7. THE PEOPLE WHO WRITE IN SECRET WHAT IN PUBLIC THEY ALLEGE TO BE FOLK-SONGS

The night it was so cold, and the moon it was so clear,
When I stood at the churchyard gate a-parting from my dear,
A-parting from my dear, for to bid my dear good-bye !
And I parted from my dear when the moon was in the sky.

" I never shall forget," said he, " wherever I may roam,
The day that I parted from my own true love at home,
My own true love at home that was always true to me,
I never shall forget my love wherever I may be.

" But I must off to Barbary for good King George to fight,
And it's farewell to Bayswater and to the Isle of Wight,
And it's farewell to my true love, it's farewell to you,
It's farewell to my own dear love, so faithful and so true."

He kissed me good-bye, and he gave me a ring,
And he rode away to Lunnon for to fight for the
King ;
Oh ! lonely am I now, and sair, sair cold my pillow,
And I must bind my head with O the green willow.

For last night there came a white angel to my bed,
And he told to me that my own dear love was dead ;
My own dear love is dead, and I am all alone
(So it's surely rather obtuse of you to ask me why I
moan).

## No. 8. MR. H. G. WELLS

### I

I do not quite know how to begin. . . . Ever since I left England and settled here in this quiet Putumayo valley I have been wondering and wondering. . . . I want to put everything down quite frankly so that you who come after me shall understand. It is very peaceful here in the forest, and as my mind goes back to that roaring old England, with its strange welter of aspirations and basenesses, that little old England, so far away now, a small green jewel in the great sea, I break into a smile of tender tolerance. Here, as the immemorial procession of day and night, of summer and winter, sweeps over the earth, amid the vast serenities of primeval nature, it all seems so very far away, so small, so queerly inconsequent. . . .The men who made me, the men who broke me, the women I loved, the sprawling towns, the confused effort, and that ungainly lop-sided structure of our twentieth-century civilization, with its strange welter of sex. . . .

### II

And then it was that the Hon. Astarte Cholmondeley came into my life. I remember as clearly as though it were yesterday—and it is now over thirty years ago—the moment of our meeting. It was at one of those enormous futile receptions that political hostesses give at the beginning of the Session, assemblies of two or three thousand men and women, minor politicians, organizers, journalists, all clamorous for champagne and burning for nods of recognition from the great men of the Party. It was a fine night, almost oppressively warm, and I had walked across the Park from Hill Street, carrying my opera-hat in my hand. There was a dull uniform roar from the distant traffic ; the tops of the trees faintly swished in the light wind, the lights along the lake shone very quietly, and above were the vast serenities of the sky, powdered with stars. On benches in the shadows lurked pairs of quiet lovers, and the stars looked down upon them as they had upon lovers in Nineveh and Babylon. As I stepped out into the rush of Pall Mall, with its stream of swift motors, I thought, I remember, of my career. . . .

## III

The crush was vulgar and intolerable.

I had spent an hour passing dejected remarks to the other young men, also there out of duty and as bored as I was myself. Then suddenly she entered . . . a slender slip of a thing, brown-haired and brown-eyed, leaning flower-like on the arm of her elephantine mother, the Dowager. . . .

## IV

" Dearest," she wrote me next day, " did you sleep last night ? I did not sleep a wink. All night long I lay dazzled and overwhelmed by this wonderful thing that has come to us. And then this morning, when God's great dawn slowly lifted over the westward hills, I got up, did my hair (oh my beautiful, beautiful hair, now all yours, my own Man, all yours), and sat down to write this, my first letter, to you. I am sitting at the little window of my room in the Lion Tower. The breath of the roses rises in the fresh morning air ; and out beyond the park, where the deer are placidly grazing, the slanting sun glints exquisitely on spacious woodland and rolling down, mile after mile. . . . Far away, against the blue of the horizon, there is a little pointing church spire, and somehow it reminds me of you. . . . Oh, my lover, I am going to lay bare to you the inmost shrine of my heart. You must be patient with me, very patient ; for do we not belong to each other ? We must live openly we two, we who are the apostles of new freedoms, of new realizations, of a second birth for this dear, foolish old world of ours." Thus she wrote, and there was more, much more, too sacredly intimate to be set down here, but breathing in every line the essence of her adorable self. . . .

V

And then it was that Mary Browne came into my life. I had known her years ago when I was at college ; I had thought her a meek and rather dull little girl, as insignificant as the rest of her family. But now there was about her a certain quality of graciousness, very difficult to define, but very unescapable when it is present, that gave to her mouse-grey hair and rather weak blue eyes a beauty very rare and very subtle. She had spent, she told me, two years in the East End at some social work or other. . . .

## VI

And then I met Cecilia Scroop. . . .

## VII

And so the end came. In those last days I worked more feverishly than ever, writing my book, attending committees, speaking on platforms throughout the country. I was the chief speaker during that by-election of Brooks's at Manchester, which I still believe might have been the germ of a new social order, of coherences and approximations, of differentiations and realizations beyond the imagining of the men of our time, but to be very clearly and very palpably apprehended by that future race for whom we, in a blind and groping way, are living and building. . . .And then the blow fell. . . .

It was a Friday afternoon. The House had risen early after throwing out some absurd Bill that that ass Biffin had brought in ; I think it was something about Bee Disease. I had been one of the tellers for the Noes, and at three o'clock I walked out into Palace Yard and along the chalky stone cloister that leads to the private tunnel through which members enter the Underground Railway station. I had promised to meet Astarte at four at the foot of the Scenic Railway (this was before the time when little Higgins revolutionized the amusement business with his actino-gyroscopes) in the Earl's Court Exhibition. Since her marriage with Binger communication had been increasingly difficult for us. All her letters were opened, and Binger had eavesdroppers at work in the telephone exchanges. Her chauffeur, happily, played his master false, and she was usually able to keep appointments when she had made them ; and for some months we had arranged our meetings by little cryptic notices in the agony column of the *Morning Post*. We had thought ourselves safe. But she must have dropped a casual word to somebody ; some fool had given us away ; and when I got to Earl's Court I found that Astarte was there, but that Mary and Cecilia were there as well. . . .

## VIII

I remonstrated with them. I knew it was hopeless, and my heart sank ; but I did my best. Greatest agony of all it was to know that these women in whom I had trusted, whom I had looked to as pioneers, as auguries of what was to be and what still will be, were, when the crisis came, still shackled and bound by the little petty jealousies of the old system. With set, white faces they glowered upon me (it was raining a little, I remember, and the ground at our feet was muddy and covered with stained and trampled paper) as I spoke, softly and passionately, of muddle and waste, of the sordid and furtive shames and reticences that man has brought with him from the ancestral past, that he must shed before we build for our gods the diviner temples that might be. . . Night came over. . . . and then, as my voice failed, a tall man stepped out from behind a hoarding. It was Montacute, the Prime Minister. " I am very sorry for you," he said simply, " but I am afraid, Mr. Bilgewater, we shall have to ask you to resign." He seemed to hesitate a moment ; then, as though half ashamed, he held out his hand and looked me in the eyes. . . I had known him since I was a boy at school and he a young man, a fastidious and kindly young man who had seemed almost too delicate for the rough work of politics. He had always taken a friendly interest in me even when I was bitterly fighting him. . . " Good-bye," he said. My voice was husky as I returned his farewell.

## IX

I went back to my chambers and told my man to pack a single portmanteau. There were just three hours before the boat-train. Before I left I wrote ten letters. . . .

# III

# HOW THEY WOULD HAVE DONE IT

## No. 1. IF WORDSWORTH HAD WRITTEN "THE EVERLASTING MERCY"

Ever since boyhood it has been my joy
To rove the hills and vales, the woods and streams,
To commune with the flowers, the beasts, the birds,
And all the humble messengers of God.
And so not seldom have my footsteps strayed
To that bare farm where Thomas Haythornthwaite
(Alas ! 'tis now ten years the good old man
Is dead !) wrung turnips from the barren soil,
To keep himself and his good wife, Maria,
Whom I remember well, although 'tis now
Full twenty years since she deceased ; and I
Have often visited her quiet grave
In summer and in winter, that I might
Place some few flowers upon it, and returned
In solemn meditation from the spot,
In the employment of this honest man
There was a hind, Saul Kane, I knew him well,
And oft-times 'twas my fortune to lament
The blackness of the youth's depravity.
For when I came to visit Haythornthwaite
The good old man, leaning upon this spade,
Would say to me, " Saul Kane is wicked, sir ;
A wicked lad. Before he cut his teeth
He broke his poor old mother's heart in two.
For at the beer-house he is often seen
With ill companions, and at dead of night
We hear him loud blaspheming at the owls
That fly about the house. I oft have blushed

At deeds of his I could not speak about."
But yet so wondrous is the heart of man
That even Saul Kane repented of his sins—
A little maid, a little Quaker maid,
Converted him one day. " Saul Kane," she said,
" Dear Saul, I pray you will get drunk no more."
Nor did he ; but embraced a sober life,
And married Mary Thorpe ; and yesterday
I met him on my walk, and with him went
Up to the house where he and his do dwell.
And there I long in serious converse stayed,
Speaking of Nature and of politics,
And then turned homeward meditating much
About the single transferable vote.

## No. 2. IF SWINBURNE HAD WRITTEN "THE LAY OF HORATIUS"

*N.B.—Read this aloud, with resonance, nor examine too closely the meaning.*

May the sword burn bright, may the old sword smite, that a myriad years have worn and rusted?
May an old wind blow where the young winds go immaculate over the eager land ?
May faded blossoms on ripening bosoms flame with lust as of old they lusted,
Or the might of a night take flight with the white sweet arms of a dead Dionysian band ?
Ah, nay ! for the rods of the high pale gods the power of the past have spilled and broken
And over the fields the amaranth yields her guerdon of gossamer, bitter as rue,
And the desolate blind sad ghost of the wind falters and fails as a word that was spoken
Long since of a fire and a blazing pyre of perjured monarchs and kings untrue.*

The sword may smite and the keen sword bite though the clouds in the sky be clouds of peril,
Though the Teuton glance at the flanks of France and the hand of Fate be a hand unseen,
For the brave man's† arm was swift to charm and the coward's arm was weak and sterile

* Possible mention of Tarquin.

† Conceivably Horatius.

Or ever the Saxon galleons swam to England* over the waters green
And over the high Thessalian hills the feet of the maidens fail and falter,
Samian waters and Lemnian valleys, Ithacan rivers and Lesbian seas,
And the god returning with frenzy burning foams at the foot of a roseless altar,
And dumb with the kiss of Artemis and the berries of death the virgin flees.

*With persistence and luck the reader, after eighty verses or so, would have come to something as specific as this :*

For the triumph of the trampling of the nations
And the laughter of the loud Etrurian† gates
And the thunder of a host of desolations
And the lightning of an avalanche of hates
Never daunted thee or made thy cheek the paler
On the bridge which thou didst hold as held the fleet
Drake, our own superb Elizabethan sailor,
Yea, and drove the bloody tyrant from his seat.

* Our mother, inviolate ever since, save for one only occasion.
† Lars Porsena in poet's mind.

## No. 3. IF MR. MASEFIELD HAD WRITTEN "CASABIANCA"

"You dirty hog," "You snouty snipe,"
"You lump of muck," "You bag of tripe,"
Such, as their latest breaths they drew,
The objurgations of the crew.
—— —— —— they roared
As they went tumbling overboard,
Or frizzled like so many suppers
All along the halyard scuppers.
"You——" . . . the last was gone,
And Cassy yelled there all alone.
(He thought the old man was on the ship.)
"Father! this gives me the fair pip!"

"My God, you old vagabond," he cried,
"If only I . . ." No voice replied;
Only the tall flames higher sprang,
Amid the spars, and soared and sang,
Only along the rigging came
God's great unfolding flower of flame,
And Love's divine dim planet shed
Her radiance on the many dead;
And past the battling fleets the sea
Stretched to the world's edge tranquilly,
Breathing with slow, contented breath
As though it were in love with Death,
As it has breathed since first began
Man's inhumanity to man,

As it will do when like a scroll
All the heavens together roll.
There's that purple passage done
And I have one less lap to run.

Dogs barked, owls hooted, cockerels crew,
As in my works they often do
When, flagging with my main design,
I pad with a descriptive line.
Young Cassy cried again : " Oh, damn !
What an unhappy put I am !
Will nobody go out and search
For dad, who's left me in the lurch ?
For dad, who's left me on the poop,
For dad, who's left me in the soup,
For dad, who's left me on the deck.
Perhaps it's what I should expeck
Considerin' 'ow he treated me
Before I came away to sea.

" Often at home he used to beat
My head for talking in the street,
Often for things I didden do,
He brushed my breeches with a shoe.
O ! but I wish that I was home now,
Treading the soft old Breton loam now
In that old Breton country where
Mellows the golden autumn air,
And all the tender champaign fills
With hyacinths and daffodils,
And on God's azure uplands now
They plough the ploughed fields with a plough,
And earth-worms feel averse from laughter,

With hungry white birds following after.
And maids at evening walk with men
Through the meadows and up the glen
To hear the old sweet tale again."
The deck was getting hot and hotter,
" Father ! " he screamed, " you —— rotter ! "
The deck was getting red and redder,
And now he thought he'd take a header,
Now he advanced and now he funked it . . .
It had been better had he bunked it,
For as he wavered thus, and swore,
There came a slow tremendous roar.
Lord Nelson suddenly woke up.
" Where is Old Cassy and his pup ?
'Don't know,' you say ? Why, strike me blind,
I s'pose I'd better ask the wind."
He asked the wind ; the brooding sky
At once gave back the wind's reply :
" Wotto, Nelson ! "

" Wotto, sonny ? "

" Do you think you're being funny ?
Can't you look around, confound you,
At all these fragments that surround you,
Thick as thieves upon the sea,
Instead of coming bothering me ? "

*Or, alternatively, if you prefer his other method, it would run like this :*

And the flames rose, and leaping flames of fire
Leapt round the masts and made the spars a crown,
A golden crown, as ravenous as desire.

"Father!" he cried, "my feet are gettin
brown."
"Father!" he cried. The quiet stars looke
down,
The flames rose up like flowers overhead.
He was alone and all the crew were dead.

## No. 4. IF ALMOST ANY ELIZABETHAN HAD WRITTEN "SHE DWELT AMONG THE UNTRODDEN WAYS"

Ask me not for the semblance of my loue.
Amidst the fountains of the christal Doue
Like to that fayre Aurora did she runne,
Who treads the beams of the sweete morning sunne.
Forth from her head her hayres like golden wyre
Did spring ; her amorous eyes were lamps of fire,
Bright as that torch their heauenly raies did mount
Wherewith fayre Hero lit the Hellespont,
Or as that flame which on the desert lies
When new-borne Phenix soareth to the skies.
Like wanton darts her eye-beames she did throw
From out her noble forehead's iuorie bow
Whose Beauties great perfection would withstand
The skill of the most cunning painter's hand.
Her virgin nose like Dian's self did raigne
Amidst her vermell cheekes' ambrosiall plaine ;
Her busie lips twinne Rubies did appeare
From which her Voyce did come as Diamonds
cleare ;
Venus' owne sonne would sigh to look beneath
At the straight pearlie pleasaunce of her teethe.
Like to fayre starres, or rather, like the sunne
Was her smooth Marble chinne's pavilion,
Wherefrom her slender necke the eye did lead

To shoulders like twinne Lilies on a mead,
Whiter than Ledae's fethers or white milke,
As sweete as nectar and as softe as silke.
O, and her tender brests, they were as white
As snowie hills which Phebus' beames doe smite
Engirt with azure and with Saphire veines. . . .

(*Cetera desunt*)

## No. 5. IF POPE HAD WRITTEN "BREAK, BREAK, BREAK"

Fly, Muse, thy wonted themes, nor longer seek
The consolations of a powder'd cheek ;
Forsake the busy purlieus of the Court
For calmer meads where finny tribes resort.
So may th' Almighty's natural antidote
Abate the worldly tenour of thy note,
The various beauties of the liquid main
Refine thy reed and elevate thy strain.

See how the labour of the urgent oar
Propels the barks and draws them to the shore.
Hark ! from the margin of the azure bay
The joyful cries of infants at their play.
(The offspring of a piscatorial swain,
His home the sands, his pasturage the main.)
Yet none of these may soothe the mourning heart,
Nor fond alleviation's sweets impart ;
Nor may the pow'rs of infants that rejoice
Restore the accents of a former voice,
Nor the bright smiles of ocean's nymphs command
The pleasing contact of a vanished hand.
So let me still in meditation move,
Muse in the vale and ponder in the grove,
And scan the skies where sinking Phœbus glows
With hues more rubicund than Cibber's nose. . . .

(*After which the poet gets into his proper stride*).

## No. 6. IF GRAY HAD HAD TO WRITE HIS ELEGY IN THE CEMETERY OF SPOON RIVER INSTEAD OF IN THAT OF STOKE POGES

The curfew tolls the knell of parting day,
  The whippoorwill salutes the rising moon,
And wanly glimmer in her gentle ray,
  The sinuous windings of the turbid Spoon.

Here where the flattering and mendacious swarm
  Of lying epitaphs their secrets keep,
At last incapable of further harm
  The lewd forefathers of the village sleep.

The earliest drug of half-awakened morn,
  Cocaine or hashish, strychnine, poppy-seeds
Or fiery produce of fermented corn
  No more shall start them on the day's misdeeds.

For them no more the whetstone's cheerful noise,
  No more the sun upon his daily course
Shall watch them savouring the genial joys,
  Of murder, bigamy, arson and divorce.

Here they all lie ; and, as the hour is late,
  O stranger, o'er their tombstones cease to stoop,
But bow thine ear to me and contemplate
  The unexpurgated annals of the group.

## HOW THEY WOULD HAVE DONE IT

There are two hundred only: yet of these
Some thirty died of drowning in the river,
Sixteen went mad, ten others had D. T's.
And twenty-eight cirrhosis of the liver.

Several by absent-minded friends were shot,
Still more blew out their own exhausted brains,
One died of a mysterious inward rot,
Three fell off roofs, and five were hit by trains.

One was harpooned, one gored by a bull-moose,
Four on the Fourth fell victims to lock-jaw,
Ten in electric chair or hempen noose
Suffered the last exaction of the law.

Stranger, you quail, and seem inclined to run;
But, timid stranger, do not be unnerved;
I can assure you that there was not one
Who got a tithe of what he had deserved.

Full many a vice is born to thrive unseen,
Full many a crime the world does not discuss,
Full many a pervert lives to reach a green
Replete old age, and so it was with us.

Here lies a parson who would often make
Clandestine rendezvous with Claflin's Moll,
And 'neath the druggist's counter creep to take
A sip of surreptitious alcohol.

And here a doctor, who had seven wives,
  And, fearing this *ménage* might seem grotesque,
Persuaded six of them to spend their lives
  Locked in a drawer of his private desk.

And others here there sleep who, given scope,
  Had writ their names large on the Scrolls of Crime,
Men who, with half a chance, might haply cope,
  With the first miscreants of recorded time.

Doubtless in this neglected spot is laid
  Some village Nero who has missed his due,
Some Bluebeard who dissected many a maid,
  And all for naught, since no one ever knew.

Some poor bucolic Borgia here may rest
  Whose poisons sent whole families to their doom,
Some hayseed Herod who, within his breast,
  Concealed the sites of many an infant's tomb.

Types that the Muse of Masefield might have stirred,
  Or waked to ecstasy Gaboriau,
Each in his narrow cell at last interred,
  All, all are sleeping peacefully below.

. . . . . . .

Enough, enough ! But, stranger, ere we part.
  Glancing farewell to each nefarious bier,
This warning I would beg you take to heart,
  " There is an end to even the worst career !."

## No. 7. IF A VERY NEW POET HAD WRITTEN "THE LOTUS-EATERS"

I

Ah!
Ough!
Umph!
It *was* a sweat!
Thank God, that's over!
No more navigating for me.
I am on to
Something
Softer. . . .
Conductor,
Give us a tune

II

Work!
Did I used to work?
I seem to remember it
Out there.
Millions of fools are still at
It,
Jumping about
All over the place. . . .
And what's the good of it all? . . .
Buzz,
Hustle,
Pop,
And then . . .
Dump
In the grave.

### III

Bring me six cushions
A yellow one, a green one, a purple one, an orange
one, an ultramarine one, and a vermilion one,
Colours of which the combination
Pleases my eye.
Bring me
Also
Six lemon squashes
And
A straw. . . .

### IV

I have taken off my coat.
I shall now
Loosen
My braces.

### V

Now I am
All right . . .
My God. . . .
I do feel lazy !

## No. 8. IF HENRY JAMES HAD WRITTEN THE CHURCH CATECHISM

Q. What is your name ?

A. It may possibly be conceived as standing in a relation of contiguity to a certain—shall we say ? —somewhat complicatedly rectilinear design—to put it colloquially, a symbol—employed by such of the races of mankind as follow the Roman usage to denote a sort of suppressed explosion, or rather, a confused hum " produced " when the upper and the nether lip are brought with some firmness—or even, as one might phrase it, " snap "—together, and a continuous sound is compelled for egress to flow through a less harmonious though undeniably more prominent organ. Or, on the other hand, its relation to that so interesting figure may be something even closer than one of mere contiguity, however proximate, something in the nature of coincidence, of body and soul identity even : in a word, it may be, or, more exactly, may be represented by, that symbol itself.

Q. Who gave you that name ?

A. Which ?

Q. Oh, no, *not* the other one, the quite inevitably discursive family " label."

A. You mean my . . .

Q. Well yes, not that all so shared, and as it were almost—if one may forgivably say it—may one ?— " vulgarized "—your, as they call it, " surname."

A. Oh, *not* that one ?

Q. No . . .

A. The other ?

Q. Yes—that other—that more exquisitely personal, the more (dare one ?) *appropriated*, the one of which, I had thought, we touched, even grasped, the skirts when our interlocution, or to put it quite brutally, when we began our conversation.

A. You refer . . .

Q. I am, dear lady, all ears.

A. To, in·fact, my—since we are both to be so frank—Christian name ?

Q. Oh, but you are great !

A. Not *great*, not, I mean, really, in the sense that you mean. . . .

Q. *I* mean ?

A. The other sense, you know.

Q. Yes, I apprehend you, but it wasn't that one I meant.

A. Then what in the world was it ?

Q. Take it from another point of view, wasn't frankness to be, always, our splendid object ?

A. Explicitly.

Q. Wasn't it ?

A. Oh no, I wouldn't doubt it ; I wouldn't, really wouldn't, let you down.

Q. Not even gently ?

A. The other way, I meant.

Q. Divine clarity ! And who gave it you ?

A. The Deluge !

Q. He was it, or she ?

A. Oh, never he, as he would himself say, never on your life.

Q. And she ?

A. She would, as she always will, bet her boots not !

Q. Not, surely it wasn't, they ?

A. They !

Q. They !

A. Oh, certainly they ! Who could have stopped them. Not miserable I, so pitifully, so hopelessly, so microscopically, futilely small ! They were all there, and there was I. And they did it, oh, quite finally did it.

Q. Who ?

(*Etc.*)

## No. 9. IF LORD BYRON HAD WRITTEN "THE PASSING OF ARTHUR"

So all day long the noise of battle rolled
  Among the mountains by the western sea,
Till, when the bell for evening service tolled,
  Each side had swiped the other utterly ;
And, looking round, Sir Bedivere the bold
  Said, " Sire, there's no one left but you and me ;
I'm game to lay a million to a fiver
That, save for us, there is not one survivor."

" Quite likely," answered Arthur, " and I'm sure
  That I have been so hammered by these swine
To-morrow's sun will find us yet one fewer.
  I prithee take me to yon lonely shrine
Where I may rest and die. There is no cure
  For men with sixty-seven wounds like mine."
So Bedivere did very firmly grapple
His arm, and led him to the Baptist Chapel.

There he lay down, and by him burned like flame
  His sword Excalibur : its massy hilt
Crusted with blazing gems that never came
  From mortal mines ; its blade, inlaid and gilt
And graved with many a necromantic name,
  Still dabbled with the blood the king had spilt.
Which touching, Arthur said, " Sir Bedivere,
Please take this brand and throw him in the mere."

Bold Bedivere sprang back like one distraught,
  Or like a snail when tapped upon the shell,
Was *this* the peerless prince for whom he'd fought,
  A man who'd drop his cheque-book down a well ?
Surely he must have dreamt the words, he thought.
  Had the king spoken ? Was it possible
To give so lunatic a proposal credit ? . . .
And yet the king undoubtedly had said it.

He said it again in accents full serene :
  " Go to the lake and throw this weapon in it,
And then come back and tell me what you've seen.
  The business should not take you half a minute.
Off now. I say precisely what I mean."
  " Right, sire ! " But, *sotto voce*, " What a sin it
Would be, what criminal improvidence
To waste an *arme blanche* of such excellence ! "

But Arthur's voice broke through his meditation,
  " Why this delay ? I thought I said ' at once ' ?"
" Yes, sire," said he, and, with a salutation
  Walked off reflecting, " How this fighting blunts
One's wits. In any other situation
  I should have guessed—'twere obvious to a dunce
That this all comes from Merlin's precious offices,
Why could he not confine himself to prophecies ? "

Bearing the brand, across the rocks he went
  And now and then a hot impatient word
Witnessed the stress of inner argument.
  " Curse it," he mused, " a really sumptuous
    sword

Is just the very one accoutrement
  I never have been able to afford ;
This beautiful, this incomparable Excalibur
Would nicely suit a warrior of my calibre.

" Could anything be madder than to hurl in
  This stupid lake a sword as good as new,
Merely because that hoary humbug Merlin
  Suggested that would be the thing to do ?
A bigger liar never came from Berlin,
  I *won't* be baulked by guff and bugaboo ;
The old impostor's lake may call in vain for it
I'll stick it in a hole and come again for it."

So, having safely stowed away the sword
  And marked the place with several large stones
Sir Bedivere returned to his liege lord
  And, with a studious frankness in his tones,
Stated that he had dropped it overboard ;
  But Arthur only greeted him with groans :
" My Bedivere," he said, " I may be dying,
But even dead I'd spot such barefaced lying.

" It's rather rough upon a dying man
  That his last dying orders should be flouted.
Time was when if you'd thus deranged my plan
  I should have said, ' Regard yourself as outed,
I'll find some other gentleman who can.'
  Now I must take what comes, that's all about it . . .
My strength is failing fast, it's very cold here.
Come, pull yourself together, be a soldier.

## HOW THEY WOULD HAVE DONE IT

" Once more I must insist you are to lift
  Excalibur and hurl him in the mere.
Don't hang about now. You had better shift
  For all you're worth, or when you come back here
The chances are you'll find your master stiffed."
  Whereat the agonized Sir Bedivere,
His " Yes, Sire," broken by a noisy sob,
Went off once more on his distasteful job.

But as he walked the inner voice did say :
  " I quite agree with ' Render unto Cæsar,'
But nothing's said of throwing things away
  When a man's king's an old delirious geezer,
You don't meet swords like this one every day.
  Jewels and filigree as fine as these are
Should surely be preserved in a museum
That our posterity may come and see 'em.

" A work of Art's a thing one holds in trust,
  One has no right to throw it in a lake,
Such Vandalism would arouse disgust
  In every Englishman who claims to take
An interest in Art. Oh, no, I must
  Delude my monarch for my country's sake ;
Obedience in such a case, in fact,
Were patently an anti-social act.

" It is not pleasant to deceive my king,
  I had much rather humour his caprice,
But, if I tell him I have thrown the thing,
  And, thinking that the truth, he dies in peace,
Surely the poets of our race will sing
  (Unless they are the most pedantic geese)

The praises of the knight who lied to save
This precious weapon from a watery grave."

He reached the margin of the lake and there
  Until a decent interval had passed
Lingered, the sword once more safe in its lair.
  Then to his anxious monarch hurried fast,
And, putting on a still more candid air,
  Assured the king the brand had gone at last.
But Arthur, not deceived by any means,
Icily said : " Tell that to the marines.

" Sir Bedivere, this conduct won't enhance
  Your reputation as a man of honour.
If you had dared to lead me such a dance
  A week ago you would have been a goner.
Listen to me ! I give you one more chance ;
  And, if you fail again, I swear upon our
Old oath of fealty to the Table Round
I shall jump up and fell you to the ground."

So that sad soul went off alone once more.
  Rebellion frowned no longer on his face ;
His spirit was broken ; when he reached the shore
  He wormed the sword out of its hiding-place,
Excalibur, that man's eye should see no more,
  And, fearing still a further lapse from grace,
Shut his eyes tight against that matchless jewel
And, desperately hissing, " This is cruel,"

Swung it far back ; and then, with mighty sweep,
  Hove it to southward as he had been bade.
And, as it fell, an arm did suddenly leap
  Out of the moonlit wave, in samite clad,

And grasped the sword and drew it to the deep.
  And all was still ; and Bedivere, who had
No nerve at all left now, exclaimed, " My Hat !
I'll never want another job like that ! "

Thus Bedivere at last performed his vow.
  And Arthur, when the warrior bore in sight,
Read his success upon his gloomy brow.
" Done it at last," he murmured, " *that's* all right.
Well, Bedivere, and what has happened now ? "
  Demanded he ; and the disconsolate knight
In a harsh bitter voice replied, " Oh, damn it all,
I saw a mystic arm, clothed in white samite all."

" Quite right," said Arthur, " better late than never;
  Now, if you please, you'll take me for a ride,
Put me upon your back and then endeavour
  To run top-speed unto the waterside.
Come, stir your stumps, you must be pretty clever,
  Or otherwise I fear I shall have died
Before you've landed me upon the jetty,
And then the programme's spoilt : which were a pity."

What followed after this (although my trade is
  Romantic verse) is quite beyond my lay.
For automobile barges, full of ladies
  Singing and weeping, never came my way.
Though, for that matter, I was once in Cadiz—
  But never mind. It will suffice to say
That in his final act our old friend Malory
  Was obviously playing to the gallery.

## No. 10. IF SIR RABINDRANATH TAGORE HAD WRITTEN "LITTLE DROPS OF WATER"

Child, I am wondering.
Last night I was watching the silver moon rising over the sea,
And in her light the colour of the sea was pale, and the colour of the grasses was dark and sweet as the champak.
I heard the ducks crying over the waters by the shore.
I heard from the khitmatgar, threading like pearls on the darkness, the soft notes of the cummer-bund.
Child, I am wondering.

Child, I smelt the flowers,
The golden flowers . . . hiding in crowds like fairies at my feet,
And as I smelt them the endless smile of the infinite broke over me, and I knew that they and you and I were one.

They and you and I, the cowherds and the cows, the jewels and the potter's wheel, the mothers and the light in baby's eyes.
For the sempstress when she takes one stitch may make nine unnecessary ;
And the smooth and shining stone that rolls and rolls like the great river may gain no moss,
And it is extraordinary what a lot you can do with a platitude when you dress it up in Blank Prose.
Child, I smelt the flowers.

# IV

# IMAGINARY REVIEWS

## IMAGINARY REVIEWS

### I

" *Prolegomena for a System of Intuitive Reasoning.*" *By F. W. Wiertz. Translated from the third German edition by Julia Elson.* (*The Channer-Webb Co., New York*).

It speaks ill for the enterprise of our publishing firms that it should have been left to an American firm to bring out the first English translation of Friedrich Wiertz's *magnum opus*. It was as long ago as 1894 that the late David Andrews—a man who, owing possibly to his lack of an academic connection, never won the philosophic reputation that was his due—first drew the attention of English students to Wiertz by his excellent rendering of the " Torso of Apollo." Since then the remainder of Wiertz's Æsthetic has also been translated, although remarkably badly. But the theory of æsthetics was to him little more than a side show. He threw great light on some most obscure problems. Unlike many philosophers who have written on the subject, he had some appreciation of beauty ; and there are passages in the " Torso " which, from the general reader's point of view, are as amusing, as well-written and at least as sane as the best critical and polemic passages of Nietzsche in his anti-Wagner period. Nevertheless, Wiertz himself attached small importance to these works, and his chief interest lay elsewhere. He believed, and he believed rightly, that there was more permanent value in the " Prolegomena " than in all his other writings put together; and it seems preposterous that we should have had to wait until he has been in the grave ten years, before getting an English version of a book which will continue to mould European thought when most of his contemporaries are forgotten. It is characteristic of this country. Wiertz is ignored and they bombard us with Eucken.

The first sentence of the book is an earnest of what follows. "When doctors disagree," says Wiertz, "honest men come by their own"; combining two proverbs which exist both in German and in English. There follows a rapid but most brilliant sketch of the history of philosophy from Heraclitus and Pythagoras to Hoffding, Herbert Spencer and T. H. Green, in whom he seems to have taken a special delight. Briefly analysing their systems, or the systems that have been foisted on them by their followers, he shows that almost all of them have been subject to primary delusions that have vitiated the whole of their work. They have made assumptions that they have comfortably stowed out of sight when they thought the reader was not looking. They have drugged themselves into a belief in the all-potency of logic and of analysis. They have been mastered by their own metaphors. They have allowed themselves to think that what cannot be solved in any other way can be solved by a manipulation of words. They have "built long thin ladders into the air, some with many rungs, but all no more capable of containing, or, rather, of comprehending, the universe than my hair is of comprehending the atmosphere." With delightful wit he demolishes " the ancient, modern, and mediæval scholastic philosophies." He quotes Rubinoff: " The philosophers of all sects have spent three thousand years burying the fair form of Truth under a mass of verbal sewage." This unsavoury accumulation Wiertz, with a grace that leads one to suspect him of non-Teuton blood, shovels aside with great sweeps of the pen and drops on the benighted heads of its original depositors.

" Down with Words," " Down with Philosophers," " Down with Systems " ; these are three of his next chapter headings. The uninitiated might well wonder why he proceeded to imitate those whom he denounced. The reader has taken respectfully his descriptions of his predecessors: Plato, " a bad artist with a depraved taste for social reform " ; Hegel, " a windbag who was born burst " ; Schopenhauer, " a dyspeptic mushroom on half-pay " ; Spinoza, " a wandering Jew " ; Kant, " a corpulent cypher " ; Zeno, " a lamp-post without a lamp " ; Fichte, " the echo of a bad smell " ; Aristotle, " an industrious publisher's hack," and so on. What had he to do with words and systems ? How did he hope to escape the lot of all the others who have attempted to " draw maps of the dark side of the moon " ? It is bare justice to him to say that he realised the inconsistency ; it is also bare justice to add that he never constructed a system, though he had the temerity to provide materials for a system that a more foolish successor might construct. But, still he did not confine himself to destructive criticism, to negation. He was not a philosopher of the study. He had had a training in positive science, and for some time he even took part in the politics of Saxony, his state. Never losing sight of his limitations, he achieved by experiment and speculation results which, whatever their relation to the Eternal Sphinx, may be of the greatest practical value.

It is impossible here to detail the way in which Wiertz arrived at his method, or the manner in which he, with unexampled lucidity, defended its use. Roughly speaking, his process was this : " What he asked, " is the usual concept of a concept ? " After examining and rejecting a number of illustrations for it he chose that of the unfolding mirror that is being continually breathed upon. By induction he concluded that if the breath could be removed the mirror would become clearer. Both experience and common-sense (which, though he could not defend it, he deemed important) tell us that the operation of stopping the breath cannot be performed by a phenomenal agency. We have to look, then (and even Hegel could not have rejected this conclusion), for a non-phenomenal, or, rather, a super-phenomenal agency. But this super-phenomenal agency can only be grasped by super-phenomenal means ; and here Wiertz's years in the laboratories came to his rescue. He had noticed, when weighing sections of an amoeba, that the weight of the sections was always less than that of the whole, and that the discrepancy varied with the temperature, being greatest when the temperature was high and least when it was low. For this Residuum, to which he chose to give the name Supraliminal Intuition, he discovered the formula : Cos 65 log 2=23 sin 45 + $\sqrt{2^{15}}$. On this formula which can convey but little to anyone who is not a mathematician, he built, by a long and careful process of argument, his theory or, rather, his working hypothesis of the Intuitive Reason. It is this process that fills the greater part of the "Prolegomena." To the average reader these chapters must of necessity be difficult and rather dull. But it is well worth while making the effort to master them in view of the bearing that they have on the concluding chapter, the chapter that is being made the basis of a whole political theory in Germany and Italy and that some of the French Syndicalists have appropriated to their own use.

The Wiertzians have gone to the most extreme lengths in the affirmations they have made with the "Prolegomena" as justification. When one says this one does not imply that they advocate or assert much that is shocking to bourgeois sentiment in the sense that Nietzsche, Stirner, Marinetti and Tolstoi are shocking. Where they run to excess is in the meticulousness with which they apply the Wiertzian instrument. Hirsch-Menkendorff, the latest of them, gravely informs the world not merely that women's suffrage is bad, that beer is good, that the government should be run by commercial men, that Sabbatarianism and cruelty to animals go hand in hand, but announces with all the air of a solemn prophet: "God objects to compulsory insurance." Wiertz never went into such detail as this himself. But it may at least be said that there is little that the average middle-class man says or does or thinks that he cannot find defended and justified in his pages.

" I am," said he, " the Apotheosis of the Ordinary." It is absurd that he should not have been translated into English before.

Miss Elson's rendering is scholarly and her language clear and idiomatic. But here and there, unfortunately, there are Americanisms that a British audience will scarcely stomach. English people do not allude to a " bunch of philosophers, ' and for " hand-grip," on page 164, " portmanteau " or " hand-bag " might have been substituted.

## II

" *The Collected Poetical Works of William Scotton.*" *Edited with notes by Bernard L. Easterbrook.* (2*s.* 6*d. net.*)

Those who know their Boswell intimately may remember a certain conversation which the biographer chronicles under date of 15th November 1774. It runs as follows :

" I dined with him at General Williamson's, where were also Mr. Langton, Mr. Beauclerk, Dr. James of St. Albans, and a gentleman from Bristol whose name I do not now recollect. Poetry being mentioned, the Bristol gentleman praised with much warmth the poetical compositions of Mr. Scotton, more especially the 'Country Wooing,' which had then lately appeared. Johnson : 'No, sir ; Scotton is well enough for a man of no learning. It is true that he is well acquainted with the forms of trees, brooks, clouds and other natural objects, but that does not make him a poet. Scotton writes of Nature as an intelligent cow might write of her, presuming the cow to have some suitable contrivance for transcribing her cogitations. In Parnassus he shall be our horned poet, our *poeta cornutus*.' Boswell : 'But, sir, Mr. Edwards hath a very great opinion of Scotton.' Johnson : 'Mr. Edwards, sir, is a doltish fellow ; and you, sir, are another.' "

Scotton at this time was enjoying a brief fame. We find favourable references to him in *The Gentleman's Magazine*, and Horace Walpole speaks of him in such a way as to give the impression that, for a while at all events, every person who desired a reputation for taste affected to praise the poet. But his little "boom" was soon over, like those of Dyer, Boyce and Blacklock, and since Boswell's day he has fallen into an abyss of oblivion far more complete than that which shrouds those writers. From 1779, when the third edition of his poems appeared, he has never been reprinted until the present day. And it may be said that just as his early repute was adventitious, so his later neglect has been undeserved.

Scotton, like Clare and Bloomfield, came of rural labouring stock. He was one of a family of nine children of Thomas Scotton, who worked under a farmer at Leiston, Suffolk, a tenant of Sir William Bolton. At an early age he learnt to read and write, and before he was fifteen he composed verses and was shown as a prodigy at the houses of the neighbouring gentry. The Duchess of Devonshire, seeing his juvenile work, sent him to have his education completed under a clergyman at Wimbledon, who seems to have taught him nothing. At nineteen he came to town with a small allowance from her Grace. After his two volumes of poems, both of which were published before he was twenty-eight, he wrote nothing of any merit. Society lost its interest in him; his allowance stopped with the death of his patron; he lingered in Fleet Street for a few years as a bookseller's hack, and at thirty-seven he died. So completely had he dropped out of sight that, were it not for an entry in the register of St. Mary Axe which has been disinterred by the energy of the present editor, we should not know the date or place of his death.

His poems consist of the "Country Wooing," which is in blank verse, a long poem in rhymed couplets entitled "Doris and Philemon," and about fifty lyrics, mostly quite short. Nobody could deny, and Mr. Easterbrook makes no attempt to deny, that a great deal of this is very commonplace. Scotton, like Burns, had a native style and a cultivated style. Most of his time he was attempting to write like the other poets of his day, and a great deal of his work is little more than an accumulation of artificial sentiments, dead epithets and deader metaphors. The following, from "Doris and Philemon," is a characteristic passage:

Now the declining fulgent orb of day
Tinged all the landskip with his latest ray;
Philemon came to seek the blooming fair,
Rending with gloomy moans the conscious air.
"Doris," he cried, "my Doris I would find—
Doris, my Doris, beauteous and kind,
Doris the queen of all our rural train,
Doris a nymph admir'd by ev'ry swain."
No pleasing answer pierc'd his list'ning ear;
In vain his eyelids shed each sparkling tear;
No virgin accents came, no step of love
Trod the soft verdure of the silent grove,
No lovely face to beam upon his heart,
To calm his breast and ease his painful smart.

With tortured breath for Phœbus' aid he wails,
Shrieks to the trees and murmurs to the gales :
" Me wretched ; bring me Doris or I die."
But only scornful Echo made reply.

This, it must be admitted, is feeble and derivative. Stuff undistinguishable from it, no more flat and dull and no more hackneyed in expression, was written by scores of men of Scotton's day, now deservedly forgotten. The whole of this long pastoral is in this vein, and a good many of the lyrics are as bad. Some, again, whilst neatly and tunefully put together, are vitiated by the commonplaceness and conventionality that the Suffolk youth found it so hard to resist and that swamped his own genuine freshness and personality. There are dozens of verses in the fashion of these addressed " To Miss L. F. on the Occasion of her Departure for the Continent " :

Wherefore, Lucinda, dost aspire
  To leave thy native plain,
Forsaking thine adoring quire
  To brave the raging main ?

Are domiciliar dells so dark,
  So dull our English vales,
That thou must trust thy slender bark
  To inauspicious gales ?

If thou wouldst fain console the Muse,
  In explanation speak !
See now the tender blush suffuse
  Lucinda's lovely cheek ;

> A pitying word vouchsafes the fair :
> " I seek a foreign plain
> That I with more delight may share
> My native meads again."

If all Scotton's work were like this it would not be worth reprinting. But in some of it, and especially in the " Country Wooing," about which Dr. Johnson was so contemptuous, another note is struck. This country boy really, when free from contemporary literary influences, wrote about Nature as one who can look at her with his own eyes and who was moved by her in a manner familiar to but few verse-writers of that artificial and urban age. It is a remarkable thing that when his thought is at its best and his feeling most direct, his language becomes least stilted and dated. Here and there he reaches a freshness of vision and a moving simplicity of speech that give him a claim to be considered with Cowper and Collins amongst the forerunners of the renascence which came with Wordsworth, Coleridge and Blake. His blank verse in places has a vigour and tone and freedom of movement almost unknown to an age when that species of verse usually moved on feet of lead and was employed mainly for didactic and expository purposes. Here is a passage to the point. It is from the " Country Wooing." If any influence is perceptible it is that of Milton :

> So lay the youth with Mary in his arms,
> Pale with excess of bliss. But when the maid
> Perforce must leave to seek her mother's cot
> He clomb the higher slopes of Haldon Hill

And looked against the sunset. Low and red,
Calmly suspended 'bove the horizon's rim,
Burned the great globe, and far and far away
The meadows coruscated with his light.
There sat the boy an hour, his thoughtful chin
Supported by his hand, and over all
The universe his eager thought took flight.
He saw lone vessels straining on far seas,
Spread continents of dusky peoples, woods
Where lurked vast she-lions with stealthy eyes,
And icy deserts round about the Pole.
He flung the earth behind his voyaging feet,
And flew amid the stars beyond the moon,
Across the threshold of the Milky Way
And on into the darkness of the void
Impenetrable. So an hour he journeyed.
Then, with a sudden start, regained the world,
And, weary-eyed, stared over sunless fields
And shades that hastened over Haldon Hill.

It were superfluous to point out that there are defects in this. There is not much continuity ; the thing is rather a hotch-potch ; nevertheless, a native strength and a certain intensity of imagination are observable that are lacking in the works of many better-known eighteenth-century writers. Here is another extract a page or two farther on :

'Twas night. High in the heavens rode the moon,
With her great shining host of starry guards.
Pale lay the fields i' th' light, so that they seemed
Almost celestial to Richard's eyes.
There where the river wandered stole he down
And heard the owlet screaming to her mate

And the bat twittering. Anon some downy moth
Would flutter like a phantom 'gainst his face,
Anon he'd hear, as by a hedge he passed,
Some good old hermit of a horse that fed
With loud bite in his dark and tranquil field.

Here again, though some might detect in one place a reminiscence of the Countess of Winchilsea, there is something which, although rather shapeless, is far more exhilarating than the endless verses the century produced concerning Diana regent of the skies shedding lucent affluence on nocturnal prospects. And Scotton produces similar pleasant effects in some of his shorter poems. Here is a stanza from "The Swallow":

> Birds, trees and flow'rs they bring to me,
> A boon as precious as 'tis free,
> That cities cannot give.
> O glossy breast and rapid wing,
> If thou shouldst e'er forsake the spring
> I should not wish to live.

And here is one from "My Father's Cot":

> I left thee with a courage high,
> The gleam of boyhood in my eye,
> And undefilèd soul.
> And now what have I? Shreds of art,
> A craven spirit and a heart
> That never will be whole.

There is sincerity in those lines, and there is tragedy.

Mr. Easterbrook has done his work excellently. In his introduction and notes he gives us what scanty material he has been able to collect concerning Scotton's life. He has not overburdened the book with superfluous comment, but what critical remarks he does make are admirably to the point. He has done a great service to letters, and is fully justified in his assertion that " In the future no anthology of eighteenth-century verse will be complete without some extracts from Scotton and no history of English poetry adequate without some reference to him."

## III

" *The Recovery of the Picturesque.*" *By Professor William Pigott-Jones.* (*Chadwick & Hopkins.* 10*s.* 6*d. net.*)

It looks as though the propaganda of William Morris were beginning to have some genuine practical effect. One cannot class as such the so-called " revolution " in designs for stuffs and furniture that has been witnessed during the last generation. In the first place these changes in design have had a bearing only upon the lives of the prosperous minority, and none whatever upon those of the masses or the general social life of the nation ; and, in the second place, change in this respect has not generally meant improvement. Morris's ideas—as commonly happens—have been degraded in adaptation and, save in regard to a very narrow sphere, we have merely seen a change from one kind of bad and stupid design to another. But Morris's artistic gospel had a far wider scope than mere suggestions for improving the appearance of our domestic conveniences. If he revived tapestry weaving, he also wrote " News from Nowhere." Over and above everything else he stands for the transformation and development of our public amenities. Here, in fact, we have the key to his Mediævalism. It was not so much the handicraft of the Middle Ages or their Chivalry or their Faith that attracted him, as the variety, colour and energy of their social life. His objection to modern conditions took its rise not so much from ethical or economic theory (though with these he was incidentally concerned) as from his objection to ugliness, gloom and uniformity. " Merry England " to him was more than a Christmas-card phrase ; the words embodied a contrast and a protest. He detested " six counties overhung by smoke," and the appalling sameness of modern dress, the absence of green from our cities, of colour from our streets, and of sports from our countryside. He dreamed of an England pastoral and agricultural, sprinkled with small towns where the traveller could find things curious and beautiful and new, instead of things noisily monotonous and aggressively tedious. Others, of course, have shared his views on the matter, but no one has voiced them so eloquently as he. And, thanks chiefly to him, the Revolt against Uniformity has begun.

We have never entirely succumbed to it. We have never quite let Merrie England go out of mind. She has been kept, as it were, like a beautiful lady in the cupboard whilst all the skeletons are at the feast. Occasionally when we have felt it our solemn duty to be festive we have shown that we still have a half-idea of what we really ought to do. I do not suggest that we ever entertain the idea of pulling down London, of seriously modifying the big results of *laissez-faire* politics ; and Professor Pigott-Jones believes that we have most to gain just now by keeping off the largest problems. But whenever we have a ceremonial holiday, we furtively draw out some of the symbols of an earlier and better civilisation. For example, during the recent Coronation festivities, the occupants of offices in Lombard Street revived the ancient sign-boards. Bankers and wholesale merchants disported themselves with brand-new and cheerfully coloured Eagles and Leopards and Three Old Cocks, and so forth. But as though ashamed of our temporary lapse into sense we remove these delightful ornaments directly the immediate cause of their fabrication has been removed. Coronation over, Lombard Street became its old and dull self again.

It is with apparently small matters like this of the sign-boards that Professor Pigott-Jones busies himself. He believes that here and now he can do most good—whilst never losing sight of his ultimate Utopianism—by studying how in small ways he can improve things as they are. "Granted," he says, "that London, as we know it, must in its essentials remain; granted that commercialism continue and that the arrangement and design of houses and streets remain what it is. How, whilst ignoring fundamentals, can we touch up, or, as it were, trim the superficies of our modern bustling city life in such a way as to invest it with some of those qualities, the absence of which was so rightly and justly deplored by the great poet-craftsman who was so recently in our midst?" He proceeds in a most fascinating book of five hundred pages to outline his own suggestions for amelioration.

Now, it must be frankly admitted that some of his suggestions are quite unlikely to be adopted; some, in fact, might, by a cold-blooded person, be called fantastical and fanatical. Occasionally his exuberance and enthusiasm run away with him, and he advocates things that could no more be grafted on our present-day civilisation than an elephant's tusks could be grafted on a mollusc of the slime. But, generally speaking, he is as practical as he is inspiring. He urges changes in small detail so numerous and excellent in their cumulative effect that, were they all achieved, they would certainly do a great deal to render modern London tolerable to a sane human being.

The signs above referred to are one of the ancient novelties he would re-introduce. Englishmen never, to do them justice, abandoned these things voluntarily, or because they had ceased to appreciate them. The reason why they disappeared is that one day a certain too venerable and decrepit sign fell upon the head of a passer-by and killed him. The small clique of busybodies who at that time ruled England forthwith introduced an Act making projecting street signs illegal. Even to-day there are rigid restrictions as to the size, height and construction of such sign-boards. Whether on the whole it is not advantageous to retain such excellent things, even though they may be a little dangerous, does not seem to occur to any of our rulers. Lives, they think, may be wasted in the making of wealth but not in the making of beauty. It is right and proper that coal-mining and the running of railways should go on, even though thousands of men should each year lose their lives in those occupations. But not one arm or leg should be sacrificed for the sake of what are called "non-economic goods." Should a stray water-wagtail by chance peck a baby's eyes out, they would at once start a campaign for the extirpation of water-wagtails. "Let us," says the Professor, "see every business street in London gay with bright signs which will restore to us in large measure both our colour and our symbolism. Let the Pig and Whistle and the Goat and Compasses be something more than mere names. Let them be a tonic to our adults and an inspiration to our young folk."

Separate chapters are devoted to various special departments, such as Paint, Bunting, and Uniforms. Whilst reluctantly admitting that the stage has not been reached at which we can expect the ordinary private citizen to alter his costume, he points out that it would be easy to begin with public servants and other persons upon whom some "regulation" attire is enforced by orders from above. It only needs to get the sympathy of, say, the Postmaster-General or the City Corporation or the Chairman of Directors of some important railway to transform at once the appearance of a large body of men who, speaking visually, may be termed prominent men. He disclaims any idea of going to the Morrisian Extreme of Golden Dustmen. He sees that all that we can hope for just now is the adoption of official costumes which may be more æsthetically pleasing than those now in vogue and at the same time equally suitable for working purposes. Why, he asks, should postmen, policemen and railway servants wear three of the most hideous forms of costume that ever defaced the form of man? If policemen must have helmets, he inquires, why should they not have gracefully modelled shining helmets of brass or white metal, instead of "melancholy blue tumuli with poker-knobs on the top?" Without, he argues, going to the extreme of equipping postmen with the cap and rod of winged Mercury, cannot we supply them with something which will bring a little brightness and joy into our dingy streets, and which may even counteract the depressing influence of the unpaid tradesmen's bills that they are delivering ? As for the railwaymen, he frankly suggests that the men at the different underground stations should bear on their persons some emblem representing the places to which they are attached. " I do not go to what would seem the grotesque length of saying that at Blackfriars the ticket-collectors should be garbed with rope, rosary and friar's gown, or that the men at the Temple should wear the robes of Greek hierophants. But I do say that, whilst retaining the form of garment in general use to-day (I refer to the coat, the waistcoat and the trousers), a great improvement in colour might be wrought and the colours varied for the different stations ; and that at each station some little badge or token might be worn which would remind one of its particular associations and greatly relieve the tedium of our journeys."

It is perhaps in the chapter on nomenclature that Professor Pigott-Jones gets most interesting. He inveighs with earnest eloquence against the naming of our streets, our churches and our theatres, our modern public-houses and our shops. He points out with great force the viciousness of the custom of calling our public-houses after the streets in which they are situated (as the " Albert "), or by some supposedly patrician name lifted out of a cheap novelette (as the " Beaumont Arms "). " Let the names of our public-houses grow once more," says he, " out of the soil of the human heart." He gives specimens, including the " Man Laden with Mischief," at Madingley, and the " Live and Let Live," which graces the crest of a Somersetshire hill. In olden days, he observes, it was the custom to name streets after some genuine local association. " If a street was small and ran by the Thames, men called it Little Thames Street ; if the builder of an alley had his attention attracted by a limping cur, we got a Lame Dog Alley, and the neighbourhood of a vixen could procure for a thoroughfare the name of Scolding Mary Lane. To-day it is nothing but John Street and George Street and Westminster Road and Ladysmith Avenue. The imagination that used to go to the making of local names is no longer present. We have banished the natural man. Fancy, caprice and spontaneity are no more with us ; or, if they are with us, we keep them well locked up under our hats." He gets most lyrical when he throws out the quite original suggestion of a plan which might invest even our motor buses with something of romance. The passage is, I think, worth quoting at length :

" With good will and a few buckets of paint our very motor buses could be turned to good use. At present I feel an angry aching at the heart whenever I see one. For why ? They are all exactly the same ! With few exceptions, their colour is red, and the word ' General ' is splashed across them in large letters. I walk along the Strand and there they pass in endless, irritating iteration—red General after red General—never a change for the eye, never a variety for the mind. Surely, now that almost the whole of our omnibus traffic has passed into the hands of one great company, the motives (advertisement, distinction from the buses of other companies, etc.) which may have prompted the sameness of name and colour in earlier days are no longer valid. Generally speaking, if we see a bus we know it is a General, and there's an end on't. It would cost the company scarcely any trouble or loss, whilst at the same time adding immensely to the amenities of our streets, were the buses on each route given a distinctive colour and name. We had something of the sort in the old days of the horse buses; the 'Monster' bus and the 'Favorite' bus were with us quite lately. It might, perhaps, be confusing to call each individual omnibus by a special name as we do each ship in the Navy—though that would be a very desirable consummation were it attainable. But there could certainly be no inconvenience in giving one name to all the buses on a particular route. I conceive that such names might be at once picturesque and symbolic; they might be at once classical in their flavour and peculiarly modern in their implications. Why, for instance, should we not have the Vulcan or the Thor running to Hammersmith? I hope I shall live to see the day when I may go to Battersea by the Xerxes and by the Pandora to Canning Town. What more suitable name than that of the fair metamorphosed Daphne, god-pursued, could be bestowed upon the bus which should take us to Turnham Green? And how intimate might not be the association of goat-foot Pan with Tooting? For the buses on the Ealing route I choose as by impulse the name of Æsculapius;

for those which go to Peckham that of Leda, mother of beautiful children. The Styx should run to Mortlake, the Polyphemus to Wapping, the Amazon to Holloway, the Dionysus to Fulham, the Sisyphus to Crouch Hill, the Actæon to Hornsey, the Persephone to Bloomsbury, the Vitellius to Eaton Square, the Cleopatra to Purley, the Cerberus to Barking, the Trojan Horse to Walworth, the Prometheus to Liverpool Street, the Bucephalus to Hackney, the Rhadamanthus to Chancery Lane, the Crœsus to Westminster, and the Tantalus to Whitechapel? Think of it—a London ablaze with moving symbols and ringing day-long with the names of the gods and heroes of old time!"

It is impossible in the short space at my disposal to do justice to this fascinating and stimulating book. It is a book that may well initiate a great movement that will leave permanent marks upon the face of our country. Once one has taken it up it is exceedingly difficult to lay it down. It cuts through shams and deep into the flesh of humanity. It has the stuff of life in it. And it possesses that rare thing, that elusive quality, charm.

## IV

*"The Seventeenth Canto of Byron's Don Juan." Now first edited and published by David M'Kie. (The Scots Reviewers' Society. Two guineas net.)*

The discovery last year of a lost canto of Byron's *Don Juan* is one of the greatest literary "finds" of recent times. In itself, perhaps, the thing is not particularly valuable; far greater treasures lie beneath the lava of Herculaneum and the sand of Aphroditopolis. The new canto is in style and content rather inferior to the sixteen old ones; and the poem in its old state was quite long enough for most people. But the excitement of a discovery like this depends not so much upon the quality of the new matter as upon the greatness of the author; were a new book of Wordsworth's "Excursion" found—even were it as dull as it could be—all literary England (which never looks into "The Excursion") would read it and talk about it.

It has always been suspected that this canto might turn up. There are letters from Byron extant written to Moore and to John Murray in which he mentions the seventeenth canto as having been completed and sent to one or two of his friends to look at. Why he did not publish it is uncertain, but it may be presumed that he meant to write a further continuation and to publish several cantos at once. And a complete mystery overhangs its progress to the library in which it was found—that of Mr. Ellis of Newton Grange. Byron had the manuscript by him just before his last journey to Greece; we know that from a flippant letter to the Countess Guiccioli which appears in Mr. Harker's collection. Mr. Ellis, as it happens, is a great-nephew of Mrs. Chaworth-Musters, the poet's first love. Conceivably this may give a clue. " Might not," says Mr. M'Kie, " Byron have had this canto with him at Missolonghi and might he not have sent it home by his servant, Fletcher ? It is well known that he entrusted Fletcher with messages to the wife and daughter from whom he had so long been parted. Is it not conceivable that the same faithful attendant may have been told to deliver this manuscript as a parting gift to the lady who had been Byron's first love, and whose image he had cherished unsullied through all those stormy years. And might it not, either through accident, or as a consequence of some testamentary disposition which may yet be traced, have passed into the Ellis branch of the lady's family ? " Failing any better hypothesis, this one is sufficiently tenable, though one may be permitted to observe that this canto was a curious memento to bestow in such a quarter. The main thing is that the canto has been recovered.

The sixteenth canto ends with Juan's discovery of the Duchess of Fitzfulke masquerading at night in the corridor as the Friar's Ghost. The new canto takes up the story at that point :

As Shakespeare states, we frequently discover
  A goodly apple rotten at the core,
Maidens ere now have entertained as lover
  A vampire with a *goût* for virgin gore,

And, sailors know, a welcome light may hover
  Above a treacherous and greedy shore,
And if you touch a duchess you may prod a sty—
  But I was always noted for my modesty.

The lady, judging by her laughing eyes,
  Thought lightly of this midnight misdemeanour,
The youth had penetrated her disguise,
  But he of course would never say he'd seen her.
But being (as you know) averse from lies,
  Our hero felt extremely loath to screen her.
Juan, in fact, was most extremely shocked :
" Friar," he said, " you ought to be unfrocked ! "

Juan, with his familiar softness of heart, forgives her Grace for her deceitfulness and the fright she had given him, and the episode ends in the customary manner of the poem. This takes us up to the fifteenth stanza. The sixteenth sees Juan one of a house-party in Lincolnshire, where he retails his adventures and is lionised in consequence. He is, for the time, free from amorous entanglements, but very nearly ruins himself by shooting a fox. The coolness bred by this exploit leads to his migration to London, where he stays at his country's Embassy and in due course goes to Court. George III's son is here treated as badly as was George III in the " Vision of Judgment." Juan, young prude, reflects gravely on the royal morals and facetiously on the royal appearance, comparing him to all the other bloated persons and bulging things that he had seen in his life : balloons, hogs, the Rock of Gibraltar and the poetical works of Robert Southey.

He goes to Parliament in the fifty-fifth stanza, and goes to sleep in the fifty-sixth, the sonority of his snores interrupting a speech by the Duke of Wellington. The Duke, however, restrains officious persons who would have the distinguished visitor removed :

> The noble warrior
> Having a fellow-feeling for a nose
> Refrained from interrupting his repose.

He mingles in literary society, which he finds composed of pretentious strutters who feed on garbage from the gutters and spend their time looking for a genuine poet in order that they may stone him. In the eightieth stanza he goes to Coleridge's after dinner. Coleridge talks for thirty stanzas :

> Juan could not determine
> Why in a land so rich in mental ordure
> Supplies should be imported from the German

Again he goes to sleep ; to wake up in the morning with the sun shining and his oblivious host still talking. Juan has taken in nothing of it ; he "departed thus, his mind *in puris naturalibus*." But he has had enough of England and, without taking leave of his acquaintance, ships from Wapping to Spain, which by this time will be cool enough to hold him. The hundred and thirtieth stanza is the last.

The new canto is certainly not very interesting either as poetry or as satire. The pinions of Pegasus are flagging. There are none of those fine flights of rhetoric that adorn the earlier cantos ; the invective is cheap, and Byron's scores off his bugbears are not so terse and pointed as of yore. But such as it is, it is the end of a great work. The lost toe of the statue has been recovered, and even though it is a dull toe it does fill up a lacuna in the statue. Mr. M'Kie's editing leaves little to be desired, but one or two errors have found their way into his usually informative notes. 1832 is not the year of J. W. Croker's death, nor of the death of Wordsworth ; whilst it was the Whigs and not the Tories who were primarily responsible for the passage of the Reform Bill of that year. The present reviewer shares Mr. M'Kie's curiosity as to what Byron would have thought of that Bill. There can be little doubt that it would not have satisfied him and that Earl Grey and Lord John Russell would have lent themselves (particularly Lord John) to his sarcasm. Take him for all in all we shall not look upon his like again.

## V

" *The Poetical Works* (*in English*) *of Robert Hoskyns.*" *Edited with Introduction and Notes by Archibald Thorne.* (*The Laurel Library.* 3*s.* 6*d. net.*)

Some time or other we shall, I suppose, get a respectably complete series of reprints of the Elizabethan poets. The greater of them are accessible in many editions, but many of respectable accomplishment and fame, such as Anthony Munday and Nicholas Breton, have not yet been issued in a cheap, worthy and complete form. With the appearance of the present volume we see justice—or more than justice—done to a metrical luminary decidedly inferior to those mentioned, but nevertheless interesting and well deserving resurrection. Save that Gillespie reprinted some dozen of Hoskyns' poems in his " Tudor Songs " nothing of Hoskyns' has been published in the last century. Mr. Thorne has not merely restored to the reading public much meritorious poetry, but, what is far more important, he has at last given scholars (who have hitherto found the rare copies of Hoskyns difficult of access) an opportunity of estimating accurately Hoskyns' place in the development of English poetry and of placing him in his proper niche in the great Elizabethan hierarchy.

Mr. Thorne has performed at least one great service to research. He has added one important fact to our scanty knowledge of the poet. Hitherto we have known the date of his birth (1552), that of his entry at Peterhouse, Cambridge (1567), and that of his death (1591), which latter was ascertained some twenty years ago by Dr. Boddington in the course of an examination of the parish registers of the Isle of Ely. The register at Stationers' Hall also records the date of entry of Hoskyns' one volume, "A Garden of Daintie Delites"—1582. What we have not previously known, and what Mr. Thorne has discovered in a stray leaf of the Admittances in the Harleian MS. 2016, is that in 1576 a "Rob. Hoskynes" was admitted to Gray's Inn. Whether or not he was ever called to the bar, and whether or not he practised, we do not yet know, and it is possible that we never shall know; but so genuine is the modern revival of interest in literature, and so widespread the net of research, that it is by no means inconceivable that this information may some time come to light.

Contemporary references to the poet are very few indeed. There are at the utmost three of them; and in none of these cases is his name actually mentioned. Mr. Thorne believes (and adduces good reason for the belief) that it is to Hoskyns that William Webbe refers in that pungent passage of the "Discourse of English Poetry" in which he speaks of "pottical poetical heads" whose "worshipful commencements might, instead of laurel, be gorgeously garnished with fair green barley, in token of their good affection to our English malt. . . . I scorn and spue out the rakehelly rout of our ragged Rhymers (for so themselves use to hunt the Letter) which without learning boast, without judgment jangle, without reason rage and fume, as if some instinct of poetical spirit had newly ravished them, above the meanness of common capacity." There is a similar reference in Clerke's Polimanteia (published a year or two after the poet's death) in which dissolute habits are also alluded to ; whilst the third passage (much later in date and much less certain in its allusion) consists of some lines of Drayton's "Of Poets and Poesie," in which occurs the passage :

> . . . He came likewise who did faile
> At making, but at duppling of good ale
> Accompted was the best.

It is, of course, not quite certain that any of these passages refers to Hoskyns, and we have no other reason for believing that he was a roysterer or an intemperate drinker ; but a careful consideration of the internal evidence makes it highly probable that in each case he was the poet alluded to.

Beyond this all is the merest speculation. Mr. Thorne considers and rebuts at length Dr. Boddington's contention that Hoskyns was an adherent of the older faith, a contention which is apparently based entirely on the fact that there is record of a person of that name having studied medicine and theology at Douay after Hoskyns' death, a person who may possibly have been a relation of the poet's but whose relationship has not to date been proved. Men of the name, as far as that goes, may be found not merely among the Catholics but among the adherents of the Church of England and even amongst the most fanatical Brownists ; and, in the present reviewer's opinion, it is stretching the point rather too far to take one isolated instance of the occurrence of the name and to jump from that to the conclusion that Hoskyns was a Catholic who (as Dr. Boddington has half insinuated) was probably involved in one of the many plots against Queen Elizabeth.

There is no documentary evidence of Hoskyns receiving patronage either from the Court or from individual noblemen. It is possible that in his later years he may have known the young Shakespeare ; and in that case he may have shared with him the encouragement and, possibly, the benefactions of the Earl of Southampton. Philip Sidney again (whose brilliant career was, alas, so soon to be untimely cut short on the stricken field of Zutphen) may have sought and valued his acquaintance. There was much in common between the two men : the love of foreign literature, the keen interest in metrical experiment and in the old ballads, the chivalrousness and warm interest in human nature. Surely it is not an excessive indulgence of the fancy if we assume that two men so much alike in character and tastes should have met in the literary coteries of the time, and, that having met, they should have become fast friends ? Is it not possible that here at last we have the solution of that old riddle as to the person alluded to in the " Apology for Poetry ":—" Now doth the peerless Poet perform both. For whatsoever the Philosopher saith should be done, he giveth a perfect picture of it in someone by whom he presupposeth it was done " ?

Space forbids quotation here from the many delightful songs in the " Garden of Daintie Delites." Some of them, as Mr. Thorne says, " are not unworthy to be mentioned in the same breath as those of Barnabe Barnes, of Whetstone, and Gabriel Harvey." They have about them that spontaneity and charm that is the peculiar fascination of the Elizabethan lyric at its best. We have to thank Mr. Thorne for his labours. Anything more shrewd than some of his emendations has not been witnessed for some time in this particular region of knowledge. The format is good, print, paper and cover alike tasteful and pleasant. This is just the book (publishers please note for purposes of quotation) for the train, for the bedside, or for a cosy winter evening in front of the fire, when the winds are howling outside and the logs are crackling within. It is years since we have read a book that has given us at once so much instruction and so much entertainment. It is a book to be read and re-read.

# V

# IMAGINARY SPEECHES

# IMAGINARY SPEECHES

## I

## BY LORD ROSEBERY

### STYLE : THE JUDICIOUS-CONSISTENT

*The next Liberal Government has sent to the Lords a Finance Bill, the only " feature " of which is the repeal of the licence duty on dogs.*

I have no party ties, my lords. I am but an ordinary private, and I hope not altogether useless—(cheers)—member of your lordships' House. I speak with no glamour of ministerial authority about me. I have long dwelt in isolation, I will not say splendid but certainly complete—(laughter)—and I am not so vain or so shallow as to think that any halting sentences of mine will have the merest modicum of influence upon your lordships. Yet I cannot but deem it my duty to say my feeble word—the tremulous mouthing it may seem, maybe, of an old superannuated, even doting, actor who has long doffed the buskin—against this measure, a measure which from the bottom of my heart I believe to be fraught with the gravest consequences to the welfare of this Empire and these ancient realms. (Loud cheers.) What is this Bill ? It is, as far as my poor intellect can determine, an enabling Bill to permit, nay to compel—(loud cheers)—this country to take the first downward step towards Avernus. Nothing more, nothing less. " But," observe its suave and genial progenitors—(laughter)—" nothing is further from our thoughts." (Laughter.) " We haven't the slightest wish to ruin the country." My lords, their intentions are the very last things that matter. Your deeds may be crimson though your desires be whiter than snow. (Laughter and cheers.) What, I may ask, have we to do with the intentions of the Government ? They may be excellent. I don't deny it. (Laughter.) They may be immaculate. They may be illuminate with a virgin whiteness, untainted with the blemishes of greed or jealousy, or hate, or the lust for strife. They may be all that. But with all the meagre solemnity at my command I ask you to weigh them, to consider whither they lead.

This, it is said, is a money Bill. It is, so far as it is new, a Bill to relieve the owners of dogs of the necessity of paying the trifling tax which has been hitherto imposed. The money can be spared, and an auspicious opportunity offers for relieving those who possess canine quadrupeds of a tax which, though small, like the mosquito, is unquestionably irritating. The Bill is a pure money Bill, and your lordships have to sit with folded hands while it passes, impotent to reject it. It is an inconsiderable Bill, and there is slight need to trouble about it. A very simple matter ! But is it, my lords, is it ? I say with intense sincerity that it is far, far more than that. It is not primarily a Finance Bill, and I would that I could honestly describe it as an inconsiderable Bill. I maintain, my lords, that it is not a Bill for the diminution of taxes ; it is a Bill for the multiplication of dogs. (Loud cheers.) There lies the rotten core of this fruit with the blushfully innocent exterior. Every competent and experienced statesman knows that the dog-licence duty is not a tax at all. No one, as far as my poor observation goes—not even the present Chancellor of the Exchequer—holds the matured opinion that a man is a fit subject for penalisation merely because he is so unfortunate as to find pleasure in having his footsteps dogged—(laughter)—by the humble hound, or his fireside decorated—(laughter)—by the comfortable cur. Such cravings have not in the past—I know not what may happen in the future—been characterised as testifications to hopeless and abysmal depravity—(laughter)—the desire to keep a dog has not even been regarded as a possibly pardonable peccadillo. Rather, my lords, has this nameless longing for the society of dumb and faithful beasts been regarded as something worthy in a man, something to be reverently cherished, something reminiscent of that infinitude from which trailing clouds of glory do we come. Many a man has been better for the companionship of a dog. (Cheers.) Many a sombre and tenebrous deed has been killed before it was born by the naïve and half-divine appeal in the eyes of some devoted mastiff or bloodhound. (Cheers.) I have not a word to say aginst the dog. I have not a word to say against the dog keeper. In my own small way I have kept dogs myself. (Laughter and prolonged cheers.) But, my lords, it is possible to have too much of a good thing. The great ministers of the past knew that only by keeping the canine population within rigid limits would that population remain a blessing and not a curse. Enough dogs are as good as a feast. If we have more than enough I gravely fear we shall be as good as a feast for them. (Laughter and cheers.) Enough dogs eat our rats. More would eat us. Once remove this tax and the sole restriction upon the wholesale breeding of dogs, the sole inducement to the wholesale submersion of young dogs—(laughter)—will have been swept away. I have no desire to exaggerate, my lords. Obscure though I may be, my only thought is to give the plain opinion of a plain man who wishes in his humble manner to do his countrymen service. But the terms of this Bill bring inevitably before my eyes the vision of an England covered with litters next year, covered with packs of grown and voracious hounds next year. We cannot feed them. The thin veneer of civilisation will slip from them, and they will become again as the wild wolves of the woods. I see the infinite thousands of dogs sweeping the counties from South to North. London will be devastated. The horror will rush over our great midland metropolis, over the thriving cotton looms of Lancashire, over the immense and flourishing iron districts of the North, a vast and portentous pestilence, growing daily blacker and more foul. The land will be oppressed as by the shadow of death itself; no moving thing will be seen save lean and insatiate shapes, which will pad along with fiery eyes and lolling tongues, exhausted with the absorption of human blood. Europe is arming. England is beset by enemies, grim, intent, armipotent. The day will come. They will spring. And when they come they will find an England, lonely, desolate, depopulated. England like Jezebel will have been devoured by the dogs.

My lords, I say nothing of the enormous constitutional importance of this Bill. (Loud cheers.) The dog-licence duty has from time immemorial been an integral part of our constitution. I need not remind you of the immortal words used by the younger Pitt on the introduction of the Merchandise Bill of 1802: "Our Constitution is a delicate and complex fabric. Tamper with one insignificant thread or joist of it and you bring the whole to the ground in ruin, irretrievable, irreparable." (Loud cheers.) I can only add that I most bitterly regret that some of your lordships should have seen fit to advocate the rejection of this Bill, and that I have no option but to back my opinion by emphatically abstaining from voting. (Dead silence.)

## II

## BY THE RIGHT HON. DAVID LLOYD GEORGE

*19— ; he, as Premier, having introduced a Women's Suffrage Bill. The reports are taken from "The Times."*

### I. INSIDE THE HOUSE. STYLE :—THE SUCKING DOVE

Mr. Lloyd George (Carnarvon Boroughs) : Well, now, Mr. Speaker, I really didn't think it of the right honourable gentleman (Mr. Balfour). I thought this was a matter upon which we had all agreed years and years ago. When I introduced this Bill I thought we should during this debate have a sort of little Hague Conference. Here, said I to myself, are the Liberals ; they all want to give votes to women. Here are the Socialists ; they've been like a regiment of human megaphones demanding votes for women. And here are the right honourable gentleman and his friends who, at any rate during the general election—(laughter)—almost worried themselves into a rapid decline in their anxiety to prove their devotion to the cause of women's suffrage. (Opposition dissent.) Well, perhaps, they weren t quite as fanatical as dervishes about it, but seriously, Mr. Speaker, nine out of ten of the right honourable gentleman's supporters, at least nine out of ten, I should say, said, either in their election addresses, or in platform speeches, or in replies to deputations, that they were in favour of the principle of this reform. So, of course, I thought in my childish ignorance that they meant to vote for it. (Ministerial cheers and laughter.) I didn't know the way their ingenious minds worked. (Ministerial cheers and laughter.) I thought that my Bill would go down like—what shall I say ?—like butter down a cat's throat. And now I find the right honourable gentleman turning and rending my unfortunate little non-controversial measure with the savage ferocity of a rattlesnake with a red-hot poker on its tail. (Loud laughter, in which Mr. Balfour heartily joined.)

Well, really, I don't know what to make of it. I didn't hear any arguments from the right honourable gentleman. (Derisive Opposition laughter and cries of " Oh ! Oh ! ") No, seriously, I didn't recognise any genuine arguments. I know the right honourable gentleman has as kind a heart as any man in the House. (General cheers.) He wouldn't, if I may say so, hurt a hair on the head of a gnat. (Laughter.) I've promised to consider every hard case, every objection on points of detail that members on either side of the House may bring forward. If you've any fault to find with any clause or any sub-section in this Bill, you've only to bring it before me, and I promise faithfully that I will give it my most earnest consideration. I'll do that. I'll meet you half way. I'll meet you more than half way. I'll run to meet you with open arms. (Laughter.) So, come, come ; just let's see if we can't agree about this business. I don't believe the right honourable gentleman is mean. I don't believe he likes to be thought mean. I don't think he'd like people in the country to say that he and his friends were mean. In many and many a humble cottage to-night, where the rain is pouring through holes in the thatch, where the only light comes from a candle stuck in a broken bottle, where there isn't a crust left in the cupboard, and there isn't even a little bit of coal in the grate, poor old women are sitting waiting for what this House can give them without harming anybody the least little bit in the world. Some of you have had sisters and mothers. (Ministerial cheers.) Surely you aren't going to let it be said that the Opposition was so niggardly, so callous, so hard-hearted as to refuse a poor miserable old vote to a poor old woman, to block up the little ray of sunshine which would light up with its flickering gleam——

Earl Winterton (Sussex, Horsham): Garn! Stow that slime!

The Speaker: I must remind the noble earl that the language of everyday life is not permissible within the walls of this House.

Earl Winterton: Of course, Mr. Speaker, I submit to your ruling and withdraw.

### II. OUTSIDE THE HOUSE. STYLE:—THE FORTITER IN MODO

These Tories! Look at 'em! What a mingy, stingy lot they are. (Loud cheers.) What a greedy, miserable crew. (Loud cheers.) The more you give 'em, the more they want. These Lansdownes and Rothschilds, and dukes, and lord-knows-whats, why, they've got stomachs like the Bottomless Pit. (Laughter.) You can't fill 'em. Here's this Woman's

Suffrage Bill, the People's Bill. (Loud cheers.) I came to 'em, and offered 'em concessions. I said to 'em, " I'll give you anything within reason ; ask me anything within reason, and you shall have it." (Loud cheers.) I offered 'em concessions by the bushel—hogsheads, perhaps, are more in their line. (Laughter.) I raised the age limit for 'em ; I told 'em the Tory agents could stand outside the polling booths as the women came in and examine their teeth to see there was no cheating about age. (Loud laughter.) I increased the property limit. (Cheers and dissent.) I told 'em I'd exempt mothers-in-law if they liked. (Roars of laughter.) What did they do ? They took up my concessions in their bloated, blue-blooded fingers, and flung 'em back in my face with a curse. (Cries of exasperation.) Faugh ! It makes one almost bilious to think of it ! These waddling old Tory members, these dilapidated, doddering, drivelling old dukes — (laughter) — they're plural voters, every man of 'em. They've got two votes apiece. (Shame !) They've got four votes apiece. (Shame ! and hisses.) Some of 'em have got six, eight, twenty, a hundred votes apiece. (Hisses.) Why, you'll hardly believe me, but there's one old monkey-faced idiot, who gets all his income from liquor, and spends it on the same, who has no less than six hundred and seventy votes. (Loud hisses.) Think of it ! One for every constituency in the country. You're all retail voters. These superior, fine gentlemen are wholesale voters. They're worth their weight in votes. They've got more votes than they can carry. They take 'em about in carts. (Loud laughter.) They've got bundles of 'em, faggots of 'em, stacks of 'em. (A voice : " Give it to 'em, sir ! " and cheers.) Isn't it mean ? Aren't they a lot of skin-flints ? Why, they'd sneak a marrow bone from a dog, or a penny from a blind man's tin. I ask 'em not to give up any of their innumerable votes—oh dear, no—but just to grant one poor little vote to every poor old woman in the country ; just one poor old vote to one poor old woman ; just a vote for a poor old woman who is sitting desolate, child-less, hungry, cold, beside her empty fireside. [Here the right honourable gentleman resumed his seat, displaying marked emotion.]

## V

## BY THE RT. HON. A. J. BALFOUR

### STYLE : THE ENLIGHTENING

*It is* 1919, *and the Unionist Government in power has introduced a Budget providing for the* 50 *per cent. taxation of land values. Much to Mr. Balfour's surprise the Liberals have impugned his attitude, and he rises a little flushed or—as the Liberal Parliamentary sketch-writers would say—" purple with rage."*

Mr. Speaker, I really find myself totally unable to comprehend the most extraordinary objections which have been lodged against myself and my friends by honourable gentlemen opposite. One might have imagined that an Opposition which was confronted with a measure embodying principles which they themselves had, in however crude and incomplete a manner, first formulated and developed in legislative form, a measure which by what appears to be common consent they do not at this moment assign to the category of Bills the substance of which encounters criticism from them on fundamental grounds, but into that other category of Bills which are based upon tenets which find general acceptance not merely upon one side, but upon both sides of the House, one would have supposed that an Opposition confronted with such a measure, providing for the financial necessities of the year, might well have found it both dignified and convenient to confine their attention, or, at all events, their hostile attention, to points of detail in the measure which, in their judgment, call for proper comment, and might have refrained from indulging in those more general observations to which the House is accustomed when matters are under discussion regarding which there is a wide and deep cleavage of opinion. That is what one would have supposed. That is the gross error—(Ministerial cheers)—into which one would have fallen. Apparently our view of what is right and proper procedure is not shared by gentlemen opposite. Unable, apparently, to vent their political spleen upon our present, they have vented it upon our past. (Loud Ministerial cheers and Opposition laughter.)

If I be correct, and I think I am correct—(Ministerial cheers)—the gravamen of the accusation against us is that we opposed the land taxes of 1909, and that we have introduced the land taxes of 1919. (Mr. Lloyd George: "Hear, hear.") I understand the right honourable gentleman to give his assent to that proposition. He and his colleagues have done me the honour of quoting some hoary and venerable observations—(laughter)—of mine that I confess I had myself forgotten, from speeches I made during the debates upon the right honourable gentleman's first and—if I may venture to make such distinctions between things which to all save the most fastidiously discriminating of eyes must seem equally bad—(prolonged Ministerial cheers)—his most mischievous Budget. I acknowledge I was rejoiced to hear these old acquaintances again. If I may say so without traversing the frontiers of a due modesty, I never until now fully realised how great a degree of justice and force there was in the contentions I then advanced. (Cheers and laughter.) But for the life of me I cannot understand why these passages should have been exhumed from the nether profundities of Hansard, least of all by honourable gentlemen opposite. What do they prove? They prove that I and my friends behind me offered a very solid and a very strenuous resistance to proposals that we thought then and think now to have been preposterous proposals, that we opposed the land taxes of ten years ago. Well, what of that? What if we did oppose them? I don't deny that I did. (Ironical Opposition laughter.) I don't think that any of my friends will deny that they did. If anybody does deny that we did I shall be prepared most emphatically to contradict him. But even allowing—which I am far from allowing, I shall come to that presently—that we have been superficially inconsistent, are honourable gentlemen opposite so ignorant of the most elementary forms of our constitutional practice, of that Parliamentary custom which in the opinion of many of us has a higher sanction even than the law of the land, as to think that the speeches of an Opposition ten years ago either are, or should be, or should be expected to be, valid criteria of the actions of a Government to-day, or to maintain that a party which has once dissented from the policy underlying a Bill ought, when in power, steadfastly and for all eternity to refrain from adapting itself to changed conditions when that Bill has become an Act? Have honourable and right honourable gentlemen opposite, political Miltons and Savonarolas—(laughter)—ever held that verbal consistency should be the primary objective of men of affairs ? I do not think, sir, that the most rabid doctrinaire, I do not think that even the right honourable gentleman who represents Dundee—(loud laughter)—would support that position in his calmer moments.

But, quite apart from this matter of literal consistency, upon which such great and, as I think, such undue stress has been laid, there is a question of fact. If honourable gentlemen had really honoured my old speeches as wholes with the careful scrutiny they have bestowed upon isolated and detached sentences from them—(cheers)—they would have discovered that we have not been even inconsistent. What did we attack ? We did not attack taxes. (Cheers.). We did not attack land taxes. (Cheers and ironical cheers.) What we attacked and all that we attacked was the land taxes of 1909. In our speeches we specifically made this clear. We distinctly and in terms repudiated any objection to the principle that the State should, if its financial needs should be justifiably pressing, absorb a fair portion of unearned increment in land. In my speech upon the Second Reading of the 1909 Budget I plainly characterised that doctrine as a legitimate doctrine. (Ministerial cheers.) I repeated my statement in slightly different words at Manchester, and many of my friends pursued a similar course. Not merely that, but, if I rightly remember, we actually pressed for the insertion of the specific word, "unearned," before "increment" in the text of the Finance Bill, and our request was—incredible though it may seem—flatly refused by the Government of the day on the ostensible ground that if it were granted legal complications would follow. Did that action on our part connote any deep-rooted reluctance to secure for the community wealth the community had created ? (Cheers.) Was there anything selfish and sinister in that ? (Loud cheers.) Still, we fought the taxes. Agreed ; but why ? We fought them for the very simple and sufficient reason that they were not what their authors professed them to be. (Cheers.) We objected to an impost so small—two per cent., or five or ten per cent., I forget the exact figure—that it produced a gross revenue absolutely insignificant. We objected, moreover, to a tax which carried with it a scheme of valuation which entailed upon the State an expenditure infinitely greater than the revenue which was to accrue to the State. (Cheers.) Our objections were not academic ; they were business objections. They were founded not upon a creed of economics, but upon a creed of economy. (Cheers.) Can anyone say that there is even the remotest affinity, save the bare terminological one, between the tax we are proposing now and the tax they proposed then ? Out tax is a fifty per cent. It will bring in twenty millions this year. (Cheers.) The additional cost of valuation will be nothing. (Cheers.) The great increase which we have fortunately been able to promote in the number of owners of land will make it a far less invidious and undemocratic tax than was that of 1909. As far as I can deduce, sir, what the argument of the Opposition comes to is

this : " You refused to waste money ten years ag
therefore you have no moral right to raise mon
now." (Loud and continued Ministerial cheer
during which the right honourable gentlem
resumed his seat.)

# VI

# THE ASPIRANT'S MANUAL

## PART ONE

## STEPS TO PARNASSUS

### I

### THOROUGHNESS IN PLAGIARISING

Doubtless the fault arises rather from lack of vigorous training and sound precept ; but no intelligent reader of the bulk of our contemporary poets can have failed to observe that their plagiarisms, though frequent, are not quite whole-hearted. Occasionally the weakness of the flesh asserts itself, and the poet will put in a line which has been somewhat altered, or even (for such is the hardihood of some) a line which expresses in his own language a thought which is to a markedly perceptible extent his own. Naturally these flaws do not escape the notice of our ever-vigilant critics. Their ears are well attuned to echoes, and they have scant mercy for a sound which has in it nothing of reflection or ricochet. Many young poets, well-intentioned enough, must have been caused piteous heart-burning by the severe reprimands dealt out to them merely because they have from time to time forgotten their " sources." We know that their treatment has been unjust. We know that they have been dealt with hardly when they have conscientiously done their best. They have striven might and main never to let roses and lilies out of their sight ; never to forget the silence that is among the lonely hills ; and always to remember that elms are immemorial and most other things immeasurable, infinite, immortal, deathless, eternal or everlasting. But they have failed ; and they have failed because they have paid no respect to the old motto, " Be thorough ! " The masters of old time were greater than we ; we can only get near to them by imitating them ; and surely the most perfect form of imitation is literal transcription. There is no need to copy out whole poems as they stand. The corpus of English poetry is very large. With time and concentration any number of lines can be found to fit each other metrically and with respect to rhyme. To quote once more from our rich national treasury of proverbial wisdom, " An ounce of example is worth a pound of argument." Perhaps—such at least is the devout hope of the present writer—the following little lines, hastily strung together in the spare moments of a busy life, may be of help to many who need but a little judicious counsel to set their feet on the high road which leads to Success and Fame :

## A VISION OF TRUTH

As it fell upon a day
I made another garden, yea,
I got me flowers to strew the way
    Like to the summer's rain ;
And the chaffinch sings on the orchard bough
" Poor moralist, and what art thou ?
But blessings on thy frosty pow,
    And she shall rise again ! "

Lord Ullin reached that fatal shore,
A highly respectable Chancellor,
A military casque he wore
    Half-hidden from the eye ;
The robin redbreast and the wren,
The Pickwick, the Owl and the Waverley pen,
Heckety-peckety my black hen,
    He took her with a sigh.

The fight is o'er, the battle won,
And furious Frank and fiery Hun,
Stole a pig and away he run
    And drew my snickersnee,
A gulf divides the best and worst
" Ho ! bring us wine to quench our thirst ! "
We were the first who ever burst
    Under the greenwood tree.

Little Bo-peep fell fast asleep
(She is a shepherdess of sheep),
Bid me to weep and I will weep,
    Thy tooth is not so keen,
Then up and spake Sir Patrick Spens
Who bought a fiddle for eighteenpence
And reverently departed thence,
    His wife could eat no lean.

If an epilogue be desired, the following may perhaps serve as a useful model :

'Twas roses, roses all the way
    Nor any drop to drink ;

Or again :

> Praise God from whom all blessings flow
> Whose goodness faileth never,
> For men may come and men may go,
> But I go on for ever.

Some readers may—indeed, very likely will—contend that in one or two places the thread of the narrative in the above lines is a little tangled, or even that many of the lines have no obvious connection with one another.

But that really does not matter. Speaking as one who would not willingly mislead a fly, I tell my brother-poets, with the most whole-hearted concern for their welfare, that obscurity and apparent discontinuity of parts will be all to their advantage. For if the critics cannot understand your argument or detect the junction of your images they will call you a symbolist. And that will be so nice for you.

## II

## THE DIFFICULTY OF RHYME

The use of the rhyming dictionary has been general for many years, and bouts-rimés (or poems constructed after the rhymes have been set down in order) have been known ever since the Middle Ages. Both these methods are clumsy, in so far as they do not give the writer any indication as to what rhymes he shall choose in the first instance. They are clumsy and they are haphazard ; a young and inexperienced poet attempting to write bouts-rimés (even with the assistance of a rhyming dictionary) must be constantly baffled and disheartened by finding that he has chosen groups of rhymes that do not go well together, and that convey images which cannot easily be collocated. He might, for example, select the rhymes " mullet " and " pullet" and the rhymes " chant " and " hierophant." If he does this he will find it exceedingly difficult to link his poem together. Undoubtedly, with luck he might hit upon a pair of rhymes that would fit easily in with " mullet " and " pullet " ; as, for instance, " surf " and " turf " :

> I would rather be a pullet
> On the turf
> Than a red or grey mullet
> In the surf,

makes very good sense, even though it be not perhaps one of the more ethereal flights of poetry. But left to choose his own pairs of rhymes from a dictionary and to arrange them himself for bouts-rimés, the poet may still find his material very stubborn.

The solution is this. If a man have not the good memory to retain rhymes in his brain and the knack of arranging them when he has them, the safest and easiest thing for him to do is to profit by the experience of past generations. We do not scorn to use the accumulations that have been handed down to us in other departments of science and art; why should we neglect those which have been piled up by our bards. Painter derives from painter knowledge of design, of the mixing of paints, and of the harmonising of colours. Rhyme is merely the shell, or part of the shell, of a poem, and even those who are purists on the subject of general plagiarism can surely have no objection to a poet making use of a rhyme-scheme that has been found convenient and shapely by another poet who has gone before him. Let poets who are troubled by rhyme, in fact, borrow and adapt arrangements of rhyme from works already in existence.

An ounce of example, as one has often observed before, is worth many ounces of precept. Let us take, for instance, so well-known and deservedly popular a nursery rhyme as:

Jack and Jill
Went up the hill
To fetch a pail of water,
Jack fell down
And broke his crown,
And Jill came tumbling after.

Detaching the rhymes from their context we get the following arrangement :

Jill,
Hill,
Water,
Down,
Crown,
After.

These rhymes are not particularly convenient ones, and a restriction is introduced by the occurrence of the proper name " Jill " at the end of the line. This necessitates the mention in our own poem of a lady name Jill. But, after all, it is a pretty name. Given these rhymes, we can without a moment's hesitation turn out a graceful little lyric like this :

I would I were with gentle Jill
From dawn till eve on Bloxham Hill
  High above Severn water ;
All day we'd gaze entrancèd down
Upon the river's silver crown,
  Nor look before or after.

Should a whimsical touch be desired, the last line might be made to run :

  And home to supper after.

We sec here that not only have we been saved the trouble of finding and co-ordinating rhymes, but that the rhymes really provided have given us a clue to our subject-matter. Yet our resultant poem is not in the least like the original. Something new has

been added to the rich treasury of English verse
Let us take another example :

There was an old woman who lived in a shoe,
She had so many children she didn't know what to
 do,
So she gave them some broth without any bread,
And whipped them all soundly and put them to
 bed.

Our rhyme scheme here will run as follows :

Shoe,
Do,
Bread,
Bed.

Little or no cogitation will give us a result like this, fully up to the standard of most contemporary verse :

Lo ! I am poor and pincheth sore the shoe,
I cannot go it as I used to do,
Natheless I'll be content so that I've bread,
A roof above, a pallet for my bed.

That is in the dignified facetious style. But the rhymes given are equally suited to the note of passion and solemn reverence :

I am not worthy to unlace thy shoe ;
Surely thou dost not breathe as others do,
Nectared ambrosia sure must be thy bread,
And doves thy messengers, and clouds thy bed !

Or, yet again, if our rhymes be taken from the chorus of a song recently popular in our lighter places of entertainment, a poem like the following may easily be constructed :

Hail, holy Liberty ! When thou dost speak
  A glory all glory out-shining all men see,
Thy glance, the thunderous perfume of thy tresses,
  Bear dreams that trample base reality !
O, should'st thou open once again thy hand
  And tell abroad the splendour of thy name,
The whole great universe should be thy picture
  And bliss make bright the universal frame.

Enough has, it is hoped, been said to indicate the nature and use of the method proposed. With this key a new Shakespeare may (who knows ?) unlock his heart.

## III

## THE HUMOROUS VERSE WRITER'S EQUIPMENT

There must be many a man who has a strong desire to write humorous verse for our weekly periodicals but whose efforts are constantly thwarted by his inability to think of anything funny. All around him he sees men who are apparently quite devoid of a sense of humour but who seem able to write any quantity of fluent humorous verse that fetches good prices. Such men may be grateful for a few hints on the technique of humorous verse construction. Knowledge is power, and it is the duty of those who possess knowledge to communicate it to their less fortunate fellows who stand in need of it.

The plain truth of the matter is this. There is no need whatever for our young entertainer to have any funny or original notions of his own. If a few simple rules are followed the humour will MAKE ITSELF ! These indispensable rules are few in number, easy to memorise, and easy to observe.

The first rule is that normal phraseology should as much as possible be avoided. Use either slang or stilted circumlocutions. A judicious admixture of the two is best. Surprise is the essence of humour, and there is no surer way of producing it than this. Long words and periphrastic sentences have, when employed in avowedly humorous verse, an irresistibly facetious air. There is no necessity for the writer himself to see anything amusing in them; he is sure of that effect upon the reader that it is his desire to achieve.

Take an example. Suppose you have chosen as your subject the death of a favourite Pomeranian dog. The rough draft of your conception runs as follows: "He was a nice dog. I had him a long time. He was given me by an uncle. I am very sorry he is dead." That in itself is not very funny. But it may very easily be developed into a second prose draft which will run as follows: "He was a hound of benevolent and kindly disposition. Long ere the days of Lloyd Georges and Churchills he was established, a household deity, upon my hearth. He was bestowed upon me by an avuncular relative, a good old cove. I weep bitterly because he has kicked the bucket."

The second rule is that you should, whenever possible, illustrate your text with any illustrations save the ones that naturally occur to you. Let us suppose that the dog was a nice dog. The first thing that occurs to you as an illustration of this quality is that he licked your hand. It would be permissible to mention this in a roundabout form, such as "he deposited lingual moisture on my digits"; but it would be better to keep clear of it altogether. Your plan is to think of some species of benevolent and pleasant act that could not be performed by a dog and to attribute that to the deceased. Say, for instance, "He often mixed my drinks (liquid beverages) for me when I was tired," or, "He could always be relied upon to make a fourth for me at bridge."

These two rules will be quite sufficient to ensure the proper management of your subject-matter, with the proviso that you always speak of small or common things with great veneration and of venerable and solemn and great things with familiarity. With regard to form there are several small things to remember. Your metre and the length of the line should be determined by the first two lines that occur to you. The key to success in these matters lies in the management of rhyme. In the first place you should select unusual words and insist on finding rhymes for them ; this process will lead to many very amusing results. In the second place you should when possible, put proper names at the end of lines and find rhymes for them. And, as a matter of general practice, you should have a preference for bi- and tri-syllabled rhymes over those of one syllable. Better than sacrifice an unusual tri-syllabled rhyme, wander from your train of thought and let the rhyme suggest any divagation or parenthesis it will. All such things will contribute to the desired element of surprise. The following lines have been constructed on these principles without the help of any peculiar individual skill or knack :

Hail and farewell, hail and farewell, my Fido,
  Most charitable of the canine race,
Surely none ever mourned a hound as I do,
  That peerless miracle of strength and grace ;
Never was hunter fleeter in the chase,
  Never was friend more jovial at the table ;
I choke with sobs, the tears run down my face,
  I mean to weep as long as I am able.

Long, long ago he came from Pomerania,
  Long ere the days of Churchill and such refuse,
Brought by a relative who had a mania
  For buying dogs and giving them to nephews ;
A good old cove, albeit of rather stiff views
  About the rights of relatives avuncular,
Who had one of those trumpet things the deaf use,
  Also a nasal ornament carbuncular.

Never didst fail to make a fourth at auction,
  To gossip when I felt like conversation,
Or hold thy canine peace when I would talk shun,
  Or join me in convivial relaxation.
O noblest of thy tikey generation,
  I am so sick that you have kicked the bucket
That I shall go on mourning your prostration
  Until my friends petition me to chuck it.

It is possible that you do not think this poem funny. Nor do I ; in fact, I think it is repulsively silly. But you must admit that it is like many others that are classified as humorous, and that with the aid of the above hints you could have written it yourself. It would be certain of acceptance by most journals.

## IV

## SOME ESSENTIALS OF CRITICISM

It would be ridiculous to pretend to instruct any young man in respect of judgment. It is impossible to inculcate by maxim, rule or example, a faculty for the proper discrimination of good or bad in literature. In that sense criticism is either born in a man or not born in him, and little more can be said of it. But there is another kind of critic than the born judge of letters ; there is the practising critic, whose duty it is to fill a certain amount of space in our daily and weekly newspapers with what are called " reviews " of books, and with articles on authors, dead and alive. In the absence of a good manual of their craft these men, at present, have to acquire a mastery of it very painfully and slowly through practice. It is not the intention of the present writer to supply that lack, but he may be doing young critics some slight service if he gives a few hints on the subject. Such hints the young are not likely to obtain from older brethren in the profession, as frank speech about their technique is not common among them.

For convenience one may make here a division between the preparatory work necessarily precedent to the critical career, and the actual practice of criticism. What is the minimum of equipment which a man should possess if he is to make a really considerable figure as a critic ? We are, be it understood, leaving taste out of the question ; on the one hand, it cannot, as we have said, be taught, and, on the other hand, tastes differ ; and, whatever a critic's tastes may be, he is in a safe enough position if he possesses the requisite amount of learning. And this learning is not a difficult thing to acquire.

A critic must have a good memory ; if he have that all things are made much easier for him. And he must have a good memory for this reason : it is necessary that he should remember what he reads. He need not read many literary works—poems, essays and what not. If he reads them—the thing can be done very rapidly, since the motive is rather a business motive than a desire for spiritual or æsthetic sensations—so much the better ; but it is rather a work of supererogation. One or two works by each author will in any case be sufficient ; but what is essential is that the critic should know what may be called the " plots " of a great number of works by a great number of authors. These plots and their atmospheres may be obtained from prefaces, from biographies, and, most of all, from other reviews. It is a prime necessity that the critic should read a very great deal of contemporary criticism. From this he will discover what various authors stand for (as Ibsen for revolt and emancipation and protest against the " compact majority "), what are these authors' leading literary characteristics (as the " subtle irony " of Anatole France and the " barbaric yawp " of Walt Whitman) and, above all, who are the proper authors with which to deal at any particular moment.

This latter consideration, save for those few critics who specialise in one author and acquire an encyclopædic knowledge of his writings, is a matter of prime importance. You must not hunt about for authors whom you yourself prefer, nor must you write about unknown men, or great men to whom at the moment no one else is devoting any attention. Very often the way is quite clear for you. The centenary of the birth or death of any writer calls imperatively for an estimate of his place in literature and an epitome of that all-important thing his "message." The appearance, again, of a new collected edition will call for similar studies. But beyond all this there are always certain authors who are, so to speak, in the air. How exactly this comes about it is difficult to say. In part it is due to a "boom" in some modern author who, after a number of years' obscurity during which but a few people have appreciated him (not including yourself), attains a sudden hold over the public or a sudden vogue amongst intellectual folk which impels continual articles about him and invariable mention of him in articles about other men. And sometimes it is traceable to natural exhaustion and reaction. Man is an animal fond of variety. A continual surfeit of one dish cloys his appetite. If he reads about Shelley all one year he wishes to read all about Keats the next year; if one year you have written about nobody save Gorki and Borrow, next year may find you hard at work on Tolstoi and Sir Thomas Browne. Whoever it be, you will always be safe enough if you keep your eyes and ears open; that soul-of-the-crowd of which modern psychologists write would almost seem to work amongst reviewers in some special manner; so swiftly and imperceptibly does there spread from one to another what may be called the " consciousness of vogue."

You know whom to write about ; your mind is a calendar of the names, dates, characteristics and love affairs of all the greater writers of all ages and climes, and you have well-stocked libraries at hand where you may look up facts about any lesser person whom you may find it desirable to mention ; in what style shall your articles be written ?

Firstly, keep your imagination and your sense of humour (if you are endowed with such) in check ; as also your independent judgment. It will disturb your readers if you make jokes ; the exercise of imagination will demand from them a mental effort which they do not desire to make (or they would be reading books) ; and the exercise of independent judgment is both insolent and an act of treachery to the whole body of critics.

Secondly, your work will gain much in impressiveness and weight if you decorate it with a maximum number of references to authors, living and dead. Remember that almost any author may be mentioned in connection with almost any other. If he cannot be brought in for comparison he can be brought in for contrast ; and, failing these, he can be brought in by way of parenthesis. Perhaps an illustration or two may make this more clear.

(1) " Mr. Timmins is a great satirist. He is in the true line of descent from Aristophanes and Lucian, Rabelais and Cervantes, Swift and Byron. It is true that each of these great masters had qualities of which he is devoid and that he has qualities which none of them possessed. For a parallel, for example,

to his subtle artistry of phrase we should have to go to Walter Pater, and we can remember no one since Catullus (except perhaps Heine) who could so suddenly etch intense passion in six flaming words."

(2) " Mr. Peakyblinder's verse has not the meditative calmness of Wordsworth's, nor the lyrical enthusiasm of Shelley's, but in its way it is unique."

(3) " The late Mark Twain in one of his books evidenced as proof of the stupidity of the ant that instead of walking round a blade of grass which stood in its way it would go up one side and down the other. We are far from imputing stupidity to Miss Chaffers, but we confess that the laboriousness of her methods puts us strongly in mind of S. L. Clemens' ant."

Thirdly, as to phraseology. Individual phrases, if you read sufficient current criticism, will come ready enough to your pen. Do not forget to use the word " stuff " at least once in every article, as: " This is no ordinary book, it is compact of the very stuff of man's existence." Other useful phrases are legion in number, and a few specimens, chosen at random, must suffice. " The root of the matter," " divine discontent," " lambent humour," " beautiful but ineffectual angel," " slim volume," " tears away shams and illusions," " haunting and elusive beauty," " that subtle sympathy which is the secret of his spell," " rare tenacity and singleness of purpose," " that vein of cynicism that mars so much of his best work," " a veritable mine of quaint lore," " decked in the shreds and tatters of an outworn philosophy " : these are but a causal string which might be lengthened indefinitely. With respect to more sustained passages, there are two chief ways of making them effective. One is to take a phrase and repeat it several times in different forms. The second is to fasten on any metaphorical expression which comes uppermost as you write, and to elaborate the metaphor in all its details. As, for instance:

"Professor Chubb says that Hawkins grafted the French variety of lyric drama on to the native English stem. That in a sense is true, but it needs qualification. Hawkins did so graft the foreign growth on our English tree. But in doing so he stripped that foreign growth of its dead and diseased leaves, roughened its effeminately smooth bark, multiplied its blossoms and gave a new vitality and a new activity to its sap."

# PART TWO

# MODELS FOR THE VERSE WRITERS

## I

## THE EXQUISITE SONNET

No purple mars the chalice ; not a bird
  Shrills o'er the solemn silence of thy fame.
  No echo of the mist that knows no name
Dims the fierce darkness of the odorous word.
The shadowy sails of all the world are stirred,
  The pomps of hell go down in utter flame,
  And never a magic master stands to shame
The hollow of the hill the Titans heard.

O move not, cease not, heart ! Time's acolyte
  Frustrates forlorn the windows of the west
    And beats the blinding of our bitter tears,
Immune in isolation ; whilst the night
  Smites with her stark immortal palimpsest
    The green arcades of immemorial years !

## II

## THE HELL-FOR-LEATHER BALLAD

('Tis a mile and a mile as a man may march
With Hope and his sins for load
Or ever he win from the Marble Arch
To the end of the Tottenham Road !)

The wind was cold and the sky was black
And the lights were ranged for a feast
When we turned our steps from the Edgware track
And faced the yearning East.

O fair is the rose and fair the vine
And sweet the sound of the lute !
But Selfridge's towered like a Sphinx's shrine
And mocked us, massive and mute !

Dark on our path lay the wreaking wrath
Of a thousand nights and days ;
But there like the fangs that a boarhound hath
Stood the challenging gates of Jay's !

And we steeled our breasts and we clashed our teeth
Though our limbs were numb with pain,
Though the jaws of the pavement clung beneath
As each tortuous yard was slain.

Great blood-gouts fell where the Circus yawned
And a drop and a drop (O Christ !)
Where Lewis and Evans and Marshall and Snell-
grove
Did keep their tongueless tryst !

The white lamp flared and the windows stared
  (Each pane was a jeering face !)
And ghosts that lurked in the doorways glared
  At the murderers of space.

But our feet were deep in the furrow set
  Our hands were firm on the plough,
And there rang in ears that could not forget
  The voiceless cry of the Now.

And the last mile died and the last hour sped,
  And as stars to the aching Soul
When the ashes of dawn gasped rapid and red
  Glowed the portals of the goal.

(So we found a fane for our weary feet
  And a pen and a pipe and a pot
And we made us a Ballad of Oxford Street. . .
  And why the Devil not ?)

## III

## THE CONTEMPT - FOR - CIVILISATION - AND - GEOGRAPHY - FRATERNAL - WITH - THE - ELEMENTS - PLEIN - AIR PIECE

We have had our fill, my heart,
  Of the haunts of men,
We will tread the stones of these cities
  Not ever again.

So I take the road to the sunset
  My staff in my hand
To make my peace ere I die
  With the sea and the land.

For the deeps are calling, calling,
  And the clouds sail slow,
And the wild in my breast has wakened
  And I rise and go.

Over the great wide spaces
  To the fields of morn
To the hills and silent places
  Where the clouds are born.

Where the curlew wheels o'er the heather
  That never man trod
In the shine and the windy weather
  On the uplands of God.

Over the seas and the mountains
  To the great world's end
With the sun and the rain for my brothers
  And the wind for my friend.

## IV

## THE POETRY OF BROKEN SHACKLES

The sun sets.
Not a breath of wind stirs the surface of the sea,
Not a ripple breaks the sheen of its placid mirror,
And the fields,
Weary of the heat and labour of the day,
Lie motionless and green-brown as the day dies
Immobile in the perfection of rest well-won.
Never a sound threads the air save the distant crooning song
Of a herdsman,
And the voices of grazing sheep
Bleating
Quietly.
And the faint murmur, far, far out over the waters of the plash of oars
From a brown-sailed fisherman's boat whose canvas idly hangs
From the masts.
High in the west
The battlemented clouds are piled
Red and purple and dark blue, all girdled and glowing
With the golden effulgence of the orb of Apollo now half below the horizon.
In the east with great strides
Night comes on
Inviolable, indomitable, immense,

Brushing wide heaven with the stridence of her
    rustling wings,
Enacting once again the old old tragedy with her
    pitiless wings,
Striking fear into the heart of man
And death into the heart of the day ;
Proclaiming, exultant triumphant, with steely clar-
    ion the victory of her titanic wings. . . .
The whole air is filled full with the clamour of in-
    numerable wings.
The sun goes down
Pop !

V

## THE NEWSPAPER PASTORAL

(*N.B.—Every other line must be in italics*).

The summer is a-coming and the bumble bee's a-humming,
(*An' it's O to be with you, dear, by the shining Devon sea !*)
And the finches in the coppice know the golden whin's a-blooming,
(*An' it's O to be in Devon when the bloom is on the bee !*)

Last year with thoughtless rapture we trod the springy turf.
(*An' it's O to be in Devon when the bloom is on the bee !*)
Whilst we watched the light-foot breakers rolling on the mighty surf,
(*An' it's sweet it was with you, dear, by the shining Devon sea !*)

And we saw the ringdoves cooing in the little vale below,
(*It was Youth and Life and Love, dear, by the shining Devon sea !*)
Whilst the East was all a-gloom and the West was all aglow.
(*O I lost my heart in Devon when the bloom was on the bee !*)

But now my footsteps wander through the city's
toil and bustle,
(*An' I long to be in Devon where the bloom is on the
bee,*)
An' the rushes are a-rustle and the tushes are a-
tustle,
(*An' I eat my heart for you, dear, and the shining
Devon sea*).

## VI

## THE POEM OF STARTLING CONFESSION

I crossed the outer gates of fire;
    I scaled the purple towers of sin
    And brake the doors, and walked within
The midnight chamber of desire.

I burnt my brows with frankincense,
    My cheeks with nard and myrrh I smeared;
    I bathed in crimson blood, nor feared
To slake the slakeless thirsts of sense.

Dead women lay about my feet;
    I trod on them, I did not reck,
    I bound their hair about my neck,
And ate their breasts, for they were sweet.

Strange beasts did lurk about my ways
    That round my throat their folds did twist;
    I drank their saffron breath and kissed
Their snouts of pearl and chrysoprase.

And things I did I may not tell
    With men whose names may not be told,
    Strange men whose breasts were tipped with
      gold,
Whose eyes did gleam with sparks of hell.

I cursed the saints, yea, with a curse
    I flung God from the pedestal. . . .

## VII

## THE SIMPLE PROSE-POEM

I sat in my chair.

I gazed into the fire, the fire with its caverns of light, with its luminous recesses the pulses of which undulate, rise and fall, heave and subside, like the bosom of some beloved woman.

The fire with its wavering rainbow tongues.

I sat in my chair, gazing.

On a sudden I heard a step, soft as a snowflake,

There behind my chair, standing yet not standing, suspended as it were yet not suspended, stood the form of a man, which was neither of earth nor of heaven. Pale was his brow. His eyes of a profundity and liquidity like the liquidity and profundity of pools in the utter depths of some remote sea where keel never swam nor lead sounded, shone with a light that was neither of heaven nor of earth. His cheeks were faintly hollowed as with the last loving touch of a sculptor's thumb, and his white tremulous lips, beardless as a boy's, spoke yet did not speak.

" I have come," was the message.

The stranger turned towards the door with a slight beckoning gesture.

I knew him and I followed.

## VIII

## THE BACK - TO - THE - LAND - AND-FEDERATED-DIALECTS MORCEAU

The yellow leaves from yonder tree
  Is vallin' wan by wan,
Jist like they valled on 'er and me
  This vourty year agone.
The saft and wistful drop of them
  Oi nivir cud abide
Syne angels tuk awa' ma gem
  The year that Mary died.

Gor dal 'ee zur, woy, stroike me pink
  'Er wuz my ownly j'y ;
'Er bore me fust an' lawst, I think,
  Ten maidens an' a b'y.
Ten maidens an' a b'y, Ochone !
  But now they've wandered wide,
The youngest left me 'ere alone
  The year that Mary died.

## IX

## THE CELTIC LYRIC

Seven dead men, Brigit,
  Came from the sea,
(Mist on the waters
  And sorrow in the tree).

Seven pallid men, Brigit,
  Cold from the sea,
And each with his strange eyes
  Whispered to me :

" O, sad voyagers,
  Whither are ye faring ?
Do ye bring a tale of grief
  For desolate Eirinn ? "

" Oisinn and Dubb we be,
  And Cucutullitore,
And Fish and Fash and Fingall,
  They spoke never more.

But each wove a warp, a warp,
  And each wove a weft
Of lost stars and suns forlorn
  And moons bereft.

## X

## THE EPIGRAMMATIC EPIGRAM

You say, my friend, that Gladstone always bid
  The light be darkness and the night be light,
  I quite agree ; doubtless you may be right ;
All I can say is —Gladstone never did.

## XI

## THE HANDS-ACROSS-THE-SEA POEM

Sons of the Empire, bond and free,
  Yellow and black and brown,
I greet you all where'er you be,
  Here ere the sun goes down ;
Here, while the sunset flushes red
  The waves of England's main,
I breathe the prayer our fathers said,
  And sing the song again.

The ancient song that struck the sky
  When Roman standards flew,
The song that smote the bastions high
  Of Philip's recreant crew ;
The song that Drake and Nelson sang
  When Heaven flared with war,
And echoed with the shots that rang
  O'er baffled Trafalgar.

Sons of the Empire, Britain's sons,
  Here, as the darkness falls,
Over your grey Sea-Mother's guns
  The warning clarion calls ;
O, and I bid you now " God speed,
  Quit you like men, be true " ;
Stand by us in the hour of need
  And we shall stand by you.

## XII (AND LAST)

## THE IN-MEMORIAM ODE

Lay on him laurel, rosemary, and rue,
  Roses and trailers of the sweet wood-bine,
Gentle forget-me-not (was he not true ?)
  And sunflowers (did not his verses shine ?)
O, pilfer all the sweets of all the wood,
  And all the musky blossoms of the vale
(For was he not the brother of our blood ?)
  And strew them where he lies so still, so pale.

A light, a light has gone, a star has fled,
  A sun is dimmed that lit the whole wide sky,
The flame that burned a hemisphere is dead
  (O, and our stricken spirits murmur, " Why ? "
Vain murmuring, vain sorrow, vain regret !)
  Is there no hope for us, no hope, not one ?
Night thunders, " None ! " but we may not forget
  The wondrous glory of him who was our sun.

*There should be twenty-four verses more (" not counting the women and little children," as Rabelais would have said), but these are enough.*

# PART THREE

# MODELS FOR THE PROSE-WRITER

## I

## THE DESCRIPTIVE-PEREGRINATORY

The sun, a ruddy and coruscating globe, was sinking over the low blue hills to the westward as I mounted the long white road that leads up to the ancient village of Molineaux-des-Sept-Vierges. Down in the valley to my left some cows were quietly grazing. They munched stolidly, imperturbably, at the lush green grass of that rich Normandy bottom just as they had munched any time these twenty centuries past. So the Visigoths saw them as they swept southward on their irresistible way to the doomed and waiting valleys of Spain. So the Franks, emerging, blue of eye and flaxen of hair, from the recesses of their German forests. So Charlemagne the Emperor, master of half Europe, as he rode quietly one day, maybe, with his swart and invulnerable train of warriors up the valley of the rapid Yolle, along the skirts of the Rocher Du Grand Boulanger, and thuswise up the little road trodden now by feet that Charlemagne never knew. They are all gone over, and the glory of them has departed. The Emperor lies—he has lain these many centuries—in his great tomb at Aix. And the munching kine remain, and the long white road, and the little town on the hill-top.

The trees by the roadside rustled as a little wind from over the distant sea breathed across hill and plain, bearing with it a savour of salt that smote sweetly and soothingly on the heated brow of the dusty and weary traveller. Somewhere a sheep bleated. Somewhere an unseen shepherd whistled softly to himself a fragment of some forgotten air. It was a plaintive air, wistful, sad, and a little melancholy. He was out of sight.

As I passed under a little archaic gate that guards the entrance to the village it was already dark. Here and there along the cobble-paved street, with its nests of low stone houses shrouded in the gathering gloom, the lights began to twinkle out in the leaded windows. First one, then two, then three, then four. They were yellow, that warm and consoling yellow that one sometimes sees in Southern countries when darkness falls and the lights are lit one by one. In a small cottage to my left a woman's shadow passed across the blind. She was feeding her baby. The stones rang beneath my tread. The world was very peaceful. . . .

The landlord was a jovial old fellow, with hard features tanned by exposure, a bald pate, and little beady black eyes that twinkled when he laughed. He had fought, so he told me, at Sedan. He had taken part in that disastrous retreat from Poppot-Le-Boom when De Lozay (brother of that De Lozay whose heroism during the siege of the Pekin Legations was afterwards to be blazoned in letters of gold upon the scroll of history) had made his oft-quoted remark, " Mes braves, hier j'étais qu'est-ce que c'est que ça, demain je serais je ne sais quoi.

Mais qu'importe ? " Twice he had been wounded, once seriously ; and on that occasion he had been nursed back to life by the woman who afterwards became his wife. " Elle est mort, monsieur," said he, with the nearest approach to sadness that I saw him display ; and as for one fleeting instant he gazed into the great wood fire, the romance of this weather beaten child of the French earth suddenly unrolled before me. Strong in spirit, grey and steadfast of eye, she had been frail of body as a flower. Carefully—very carefully—he had tended her, watching in agony as those sweet and wan and uncomplaining features grew tenser and whiter under the cruel hand of death. And at last she had gone and left him alone. Somewhere, I knew, in this old, rambling house with its low ceilings and its heavy furniture of oak, was a room consecrated to her memory, a room where the yellow blinds were always drawn, where a four-poster bed slept under a quiet old counterpane of silk, where an old dress or two, maybe, hung undisturbed on the hooks on which their wearer long ago had placed them, where a faint scent of dead rose-leaves and lavender vaguely pervaded the air.

I went to bed and slept the sleep of the just. No dreams broke in on the sleep that the kindly god shed like a dew upon my tired body. The first thing of which I was conscious was the little maid-servant's charming pipe, " Voici d'eau chaud de m'sieu.." Somewhat leisurely I dressed, content with myself and the world. Was it a mean thing to have traversed all France from the Val du Piou-Piou over the broad plains of the Bobais and the Pimpaigne, to have forded deep rivers and scaled high mountains, until here I was at last at the head of the Yolle Valley and with my face set towards the Sarche estuary and the Ile d'O ?

I ate an enormous breakfast, settled my bill, strapped my knapsack to my back, and emerged through the cool porch into the steep street already hot from the steady smiting of the morning sun. It had been empty at night ; it was little more populous in the full blaze of day. A group of idle, sunburnt women stood placidly gossiping in a doorway ; three scraggy fowls scratched the ground and pecked after the manner of their kind ; a mongrel puppy, very concentrated on his work, nosed about in a small but evil-smelling heap of rubbish outside the old church that had been built by a pious twelfth-century crusader home from the wars around the Sepulchre of Christ.

Out of the higher gate, a low arch in the crumbling and lizard-haunted wall, a magnificent prospect met my eyes. The slope had been very abrupt, and by mounting a little rock at the side of the road I could look right down over the village and along the valley to the plains from which I had come. There in the foreground was the church tower. Beyond it was the declivity up which the road climbed. And then, with the Yolle a silver ribbon in the nearer distance, miles beyond miles of wooded pastures, mottled with grazing flocks and stretching away into the bluish haze of the southern provinces. There was no one on the road. The world was very quiet.

Somewhere out of sight a shepherd whistled a fragment from some long-forgotten song.

## THE ASPIRANT'S MANUAL

## II

## THE CENTENARY-ESTIMATORY

It is a hundred years to-day since Estcourt Peakyblinder, one of the most puzzling and at the same time most fascinating figures in nineteenth-century literary history, was born, and almost fifty since he died. During that period what storms have raged around his personality and his work, what lava-streams of savage denunciation, what glittering floods of unrestrained panegyric have been provoked by them ! Old men still living remember the fierce controversy that broke out when he published "The Tragedy of Ghenghis Khan." England was rent in twain by it, and for months it was scarcely safe for a known friend of Peakyblinder's to show himself in the street. Another tumult, hardly less violent, burst forth in the early eighties when Mrs. Pipkin Pooke published her collection of letters. Those letters, which threw a blaze of light upon the hitherto obscure question of the poet's relations with Sophonisba Sock, his first love, with the famous Mrs. Perkinson, and with the infamous Aurelia Mumpson, were for a whole year the subject of a literary war of unprecedented ferocity, with Blair of *The Weekly Periodical* on one side and the doughty Limpetter and the brilliant staff he had gathered around him on *The Sempiternal Review* on the other. The echoes of that battle have not yet died down. It is possible that they will never entirely die down. But we have got perhaps far enough away from the pristine heats of the fray to survey the subject calmly and dispassionately. As Professor Algernon Jones so penetratingly says in his recent informative study, " We do not at this time of day think with Blair that Peakyblinder was a monster, nor, on the other hand, can we entirely countenance the view of Limpetter that he was a saint. Would it not be truer to say that he was just an ordinary man, not all bad and not all good, common clay illuminated with something of the divine fire, wilful yet lovable (perhaps for the very reason that he was wilful), son of our ancient mother earth, erring, assoiled with dross, yet ' trailing clouds of glory ' from that ineffable beyond which was his spirit's home ? " And after all, what do the details of such a man's daily life matter to us ? Were it not savouring of ingratitude if we should prolong wordy warfare over the dead deeds of one who has left us so much that is priceless and immortal ?

For regarding the permanent value of the bulk of his work there can now be no dispute. The consensus of modern opinion is at one with Peakyblinder's contemporaries in condemning as dull and lacking in the true flame of inspiration " Herodotus at Halicarnassus," the " Hebdomadal Hemistiches," and the majority of the sonnets of the middle period. Most of these works were written (though in some cases only in rough draft) during the poet's two visits to Dongola, when, as is well known, a strange lassitude oppressed him, and he usually had to use physical force to compel himself to take up the pen. For a different reason we could most of us do without certain of the lyrics and some passages in " The Tragedy of Ghenghis Khan." The outcry against this latter play at the time of its publication was certainly an exaggerated one. In some of the verses to which most exception was taken at the time the modern eye finds it hard indeed to detect the causes of offence. What reader to-day, for instance, can understand how our mid-Victorian predecessors found flagrant indecency in such lines as:

> "The moon
> Unveils her argent bosom to the sky";

or religious heterodoxy in Sigismund's despairing cry:

> "Yea, natheless, but I will
> Tear down the towering heavens from their seat."

But in many instances the accusations were all too true. No one can read such things as the second and fourth stanzas (one forbears from quoting them) of "Pan to Aphrodite," or the middle section of "Campaspe," or (disgusting in a different way) the terrible "Threnody of Tumours" without experiencing a blush of shame that such loathsome excrescences should have blotched the matchless fame of a Peakyblinder. He might well have left such work to lesser men.

Yet think of the treasures, serene and undefiled, that we have to set over against all this! Peakyblinder possessed in supreme, in unparalleled, measure two great gifts. No other English poet—saving always Shakespeare—has had his power of rending, as it were, the veil from the human soul at its moments of greatest intensity. He considered (as the old Latin tag one used to learn at school had it) nothing alien to him that was human ; but the great, gripping crises of the emotions and the spirit were his own peculiar province. Scene after scene from the crucial acts of his dramas has already passed into the region where it is above and beyond criticism. Such scenes as that in which Mercia, maddened with blood, nails the dead Cicero's tongue to the rostrum which but a few years before had rung with his glowing perorations, are already classics. "Red tongue, talk through thy blood," she says. Even at the hundredth time of repeating, the terse, blazingly savage and significant words never fail to produce their thrill. The same gift is illustrated again and again in the lyrics. Little scarlet cameos they are, each one impregnated with some essential aspect of the tortured human soul. Quotations were superfluous. Why quote what all must be familiar with ?

And the second great gift with which the gods at his birth endowed Estcourt Peakyblinder was the gift of music. Mr. T. Le Page Jiggins, in his "Reminiscenses of a Busy Life," states (and the statement has gained wide currency) that Gollock, the novelist, who at one time was among Peakyblinder's most intimate associates, told him on more than one occasion that the poet was entirely unsusceptible to vocal and instrumental music. He repeats, moreover, an anecdote (which in my opinion is of at least doubtful authenticity) to the effect that Henry Bell, the critic, and Theophilus Boo, the Dutch Liberal statesman (at that time on a visit to this country, of which his mother was a native, though born of

Dutch parents), once took Peakyblinder to a People's Concert at the Crystal Palace (then newly opened), and that at the close of the evening the author of "Genghis Khan" quite innocently asked the astonished Boo whether an oboe was the same thing as an organ. This is scarcely credible; but it seems established beyond possibility of denial that Peakyblinder had not what is commonly called an "ear for music." Nevertheless, paradoxical though the assertion may seem, he was perhaps the most illustrious musician that England has ever produced. He was master of the whole range of harmony and melody. He knew how to sweep men off their feet with a resistless pæan of gladness pouring along with great clashes and crashes of cunningly orchestrated sound. Now he throbs forth some rolling funeral march, thunderous with the footsteps of the timeless dead; now he sighs some sad and intangible melody in a minor key; and anon he is making us move our feet to the lilt of some merry dance tune that Rameau or Strauss might have written. Truly he was one of the greatest musicians that ever lived. But his materials were not sharps and flats but consonants and vowels, not triplets and tied minims but anapæsts and spondees. It is well that on this his hundredth anniversary England should lay a chaplet of laurel on his grave.

## III

## THE SOUL-OF-A-FOREIGN-CAPITAL SPECIES

Bangkok is the city of a dream. She dreams her timeless dream at the gate of the desert. The centuries have rolled over her, the legions of conqueror after conqueror have trampled her underfoot, but the old city remains as she was, clad in the shadowy and iridescent hues of the twilight and the dawn, wearing her old inscrutable smile. Her tall towers have been hurled to the ground, her streets have run with blood, fire has blackened and scarred her ; but always she has risen again from her ashes, unchanged, yet the same. Her body has been ravished and defiled, but her soul, after two thousand years, is still virginal and unspotted. Veiled in the impenetrable yet impalpable wrappings of her sphinx-like mystery, lonely, mournful, all-wise, all-sorrowful, she rises a spiritual thing between the illimitable sands and that sacred, softly flowing river the source of which no man knows, a city apart, a being not of time but of eternity.

One reaches Bangkok by Penoccident line from Marseilles. The overland route is difficult, dangerous, infested with brigands, and expensive, and takes forty-two days longer to traverse than that by sea. For practical purposes, therefore, it is out of the question. The boats, though small, are comfortable and fast. Twenty-three days after eating your breakfast in Paris you enter the estuary of the Ho-Hum, and six hours more, steaming with the tide, finds the vessel slowly heaving to at the great stone quay under the shadow of the principal mosque. The scene as one disembarks is one of incredible confusion. Bells clang, cannon boom, a horde of dusky porters rush about with one's luggage, shouting in a babel of discordant tongues, excited vendors of shawls, sweetmeats, metalwork, and the thousand and one other trifles that appeal to the heart of the traveller, scurry hither and thither, gesticulating wildly and chattering like an army of monkeys. Here and there is a woman veiled from head to foot, gazing at one with great black eyes through the holes in the tarboosh that the Sufi religion ordains for every woman when she is outside the kraal of her lord and master ; and at the back of the crowd stand, pensive and gloomy, a group of beetle-browed priests with flowing beards and quaint triangular caps (not unlike a species of elongated dahabiyeh) upon their heads. We have left the West behind us. Here in this fantastic town, with its minarets and its cupolas, its narrow streets of blank white walls, its rice bazaars and its extraordinary blaze of bright colours, we have crossed the threshold into another world. We have left behind us the world of hurry and bustle, of tramcars and electric light, of post offices and public-houses, of sewers and suffragettes, and entered a realm where nothing has altered since the birth of time, and where every fairy tale comes true.

Needless to say, the hotel accommodation is not of the best. The principal establishments—the

Hotel de Londres and the Hotel Asquith—face one another across the principal square. Neither of them can boast more than twenty bedrooms, and at the former, where my wife and I stayed, there was not even a bath to be procured save in the large tank in the courtyard that did duty as a recreation ground for the pack elephants that came across the desert from Abyssinia with the numerous caravans. The proprietor, a stoutish, yellow gentleman with the euphonious name of Chook, knew a little English. In early life he had (so he told me) been a member of a troupe of jugglers that had toured through Europe, including the British Isles. He knew Edinburgh, Glasgow, Leeds, Stow-in-the-Wold, and, of course, London. But as the vocabulary which he had acquired was mostly of a denunciatory and imprecatory character it was not of very much assistance. Happily my wife bethought her of a visit to the British Consul. He, poor man, was delighted to see us, as no British tourists had visited the city—(" infernal hole," he called it)—since the beginning of the last rainy season. After giving me a glass of really excellent whisky, he proceeded with the utmost despatch to send for an interpreter. In five minutes the man arrived. Like the rest of his nationality, he turned out to be a most arrant swindler. We knew, though the knowledge was of little avail to us, as we were helpless in his hands, that he cheated us most outrageously whenever he made a purchase on our behalf. But that is the price the traveller in strange places of the earth must always expect to pay for the satisfaction of his curiosity ;

and after all, we might have gone farther and fared much worse, for Abdul Gomez, though he himself defrauded us right and left, would never allow anyone else to do so. Once at least he proved a very present help in time of trouble. My wife, when speeding along in a rickshaw, had accidentally thrown a banana skin in the face of a wooden deity that happened at that moment to be passing along the street with a procession of ragged devotees. It seemed for a few anxious moments as though we were going to be the central figures of an ugly street row. Things had already taken an awkward turn, and the leader of the mob was ominously sharpening his wicked-looking curved yashmak when Abdul arrived upon the scene, and, by explaining briefly that we were English, speedily cleared up the misunderstanding.

Wonderful though this dream city of the East is at all times, it is perhaps at the annual festival that it is most alluring, most challenging, most marvellous of all. The festival is held in honour of the goddess Quog (properly speaking, the goddess of toads, though it may be doubted whether one modern Bangkokian in a thousand knows of the lady's association with those unattractive animals), and for a whole week the population, men, women, and children, give themselves up to a delirious riot of worship and amusement. All the houses are gaily draped with silk hangings—green, yellow, red, blue, orange, indigo and violet. Flags stream merrily from every flagpole ; triumphal arches guard the entrance to every street, even in the humblest quarters ; dancing, singing and praying go on incessantly from morning till sundown, and the purveyors of fruit and cooling drinks drive a roaring trade. As evening falls a thousand heavy and intoxicating odours rise from streets and river. The songs subside, the noise of the dancing feet is gradually stilled, the Present fades away, the Past comes out, spreading great wings, and broods over the great city. Night and the eternities have reasserted their sway. The heat and excitement of the joyous day have, dying, left behind them a subtle essence that gives the key to much that one had not understood in the character and religion of this strange people. The flames on the roofs of the goddess' temple sink and die away; the smoke floats off and is dispelled; nothing breaks the stillness save the wail of some river bird and the weak cry of a new-born babe. Here, under the alien stars of this alien sky, the great processes of life are going on and will not be denied.

That was ten years ago. Probably if I went back to Bangkok to-day I should find the railway there and taxi-cabs awaiting arrivals at the station, and lifts in all the houses, and French bookshops and cookshops in the great square. The clamorous West will invade the place—may have invaded it already; iron and electricity and steam and "education" will shatter the fair illusions that have survived countless centuries of storm and stress. Yet even now, I fancy, to the man of seeing eye and understanding heart the old, dreamy Bangkok, all-wise, all-sorrowful, swathed in her garments of starshine and the declining sun's last ineluctable breath, will reveal herself as of old—a symbol, a spirit, a reminder of things too deep for tears, a monument more perennial than brass.

## IV

## THE PRETTY FABLE

The sun beat down pitilessly. The illimitable sands stretched out tawny and blindingly hot to the horizon. The blue sky trembled and burned with a fierceness that seemed as if it could never be dimmed.

The Man toiled on beneath his load. How long had he been walking thus over these parched wastes? Centuries, thousands of years, perhaps . . . he had lost all count of time. He could not remember the days when he had been free. It seemed to him as though from the dawn of the world he had been treading the sands, scorched by the rays of that torrid sun and mocked by the intense blue of that yawning gulf over his head. His back bent beneath his burden and great gouts of sweat gathered on his brow and rolled down his furrowed cheek.

No, there was no hope. For thousands of years he had been alone. Every century at sunset a Shape had passed him. One had passed him yesterday. He had held out pleading hands to it, but his reward had been gibes of scorn. And every Shape as it swept past him had added to his load!

One came and put an Island on his back, and one a Sea. One had burdened him with a Yoke of Oxen, and one with a Great Cheese. There had come a gaunt Shape, more horrible than the others, and he had brought in his hand for addition to the man's burden a Great Ship with sides of iron and a heart of iron; and another, whose teeth were made of diamonds and his nose of a single pearl, had flung on the bowed shoulders the Corpse of a Butterfly.

He was very weary.

Mile after mile he walked on, looking neither to the right hand nor to the left. His eyes were leaden in their hue, like the eyes of sick cattle. His brow, lined and scored with the furrows of ages, streamed with Great Gouts of Sweat. Over his bare shoulders fell a few grey and mud-stained locks, ragged and pathetic, but still unkempt. His chest and feet were bare, also his poor feet, that were bruised and bleeding with the long journey; and round his loins was a wisp of cloth.

But Resolution was in his heart.

It chanced that, toiling on over the hot sands, he espied a Rock by the wayside. He was very weary. With an effort—for he had become so accustomed to walking in a straight line that he could scarcely compel his feet to turn aside from the direct track—he turned aside and sought its shelter. For it was very hot.

He lay down.

And as he lay down, with his burden still clinging to his shoulders, it happened that he fell into a sleep. He was very weary, and his sleep was profound. And as he lay in a profound sleep it happened that he fell into a dream.

He dreamt that he was in a great forest, a forest that had never been penetrated by the light of the sun. Giant writhing creepers stretched from tree to tree. The trees were ancient and their trunks massive. How lofty they were he could not tell, for the darkness was such and the density of their foliage such that he could not see their tops. In his dream he saw himself lying, bound hand and foot, at the base of one of the largest trees in the forest. How long he had been there he did not know. It might have been centuries, it might have been thousands of years. As his eyes became more accustomed to the strange light he noticed that he was not alone. There, right in front of him, at the base of the next tree, gleamed two eyes, as red as live coals, in a form vague but horrible.

The eyes looked at him. They fascinated him. He could not take his eyes off them. They seemed to burn and bore their way into the deepest recesses and caverns of his soul. And they seemed to speak to him.

At first, for all his straining, the Man could not penetrate the meaning of the words. They came floating to him, vague and unintelligible as words in a dream, which indeed they were. "Oh," he thought, "that I could understand!" But he could not understand. And his dream shivered and ended.

And again he dreamt. This time he lay in a reedy marsh by the brink of a great lake. The reeds were around and about him, but through their waving tops he could perceive patches of a twilight sky, cloudy, yet clean and star-sprinkled between the interstices of the clouds. The wind sighed and the reeds rustled, and instinctively he made a movement with his hands. To his surprise, though he knew not why he should be astonished at it, he found that his hands were free. He felt over his body, his poor, wasted body, and he knew that it was his own. But when he felt his feet they were firmly bound, and he could not release them. And suddenly he knew that he was not alone. There, right in front of him, were two eyes. They were bright, but they did not burn ; they glowed, but with the radiance not of a furnace, but of a large and lustrous moon. And as he looked he knew that the eyes were speaking to him.

At first he could not hear the words aright. They were strange and foreign, like words in a dream, which, indeed, they were. But as, leaning forward with his ears straining and all his strength concentrated on the task, he listened and listened to the syllables which were repeated again and again like the syllables in some magic incantation, he heard, at first indistinctly, then more plainly, the words that the eyes were speaking.

" You are afraid," they said.

And again his dream was shattered, and again he dreamed. He lay in an open meadow under a sky of dawn. Not a cloud marred the placid surface of the heavens, and though the light of morning had half flooded the sky, a few large stars still gleamed in the ineffable vault. He felt happy, he knew not why ; but when he felt his body he knew. His hands and his feet also were free ; his strength had returned to him ; his thews and sinews were robust and braced as in a youth that he had long forgotten ; he sighed contentedly and stretched himself, his breast gently heaving with some mysterious sense as of freedom new-won and a world new-conquered. And as he lay and stretched himself he knew that he was not alone.

There, standing on the grass right in front of him,

stood a Being in form and feature like a man but more glorious. His long garment without seam fell in a gracious curve from his neck to his feet. His brow was calm and his lips curved in a faint and beatific smile. But his eyes were wonderful, and shone like the fading stars. And as the man looked at him it seemed as though the eyes spoke.

And he knew what they said at once, without doubt or hesitation. This was their message : " You are not afraid."

And the Man rose and stretched his arms towards the rim of the golden sun now appearing over the edge of the world. He cried aloud in the strength of his joy and his new-won freedom. And as he cried there blew a little wind ; and as the wind blew there came from the far away a little voice, a still small voice no bigger than a man's hand.

And the voice whispered : " You have conquered."

And the Man fell down, and the Woman danced on his Chest.

## VI

## THE TURKEY CARPET

(OR " SEE HOW MANY AUTHORS *I* CAN MENTION ! ")

" Life was built for them, not on the hope of a Hereafter, but on the proud self-consciousness of noble souls." Thus J. R. Green of the Anglo-Saxons. The gifted historian of the English people summarises in this one brief sentence the whole spiritual and mental outlook of a people. It is an outlook very distinct and clear-cut, but an outlook from which we of the twentieth century have moved far indeed. It is difficult perhaps to define the distinction with any degree of exactitude. One remembers the philosopher in " Rasselas." " Deviation from nature is deviation from happiness," said he. " Let me only know what it is to live according to nature," observed the much-impressed Rasselas. " To live according to nature," replied the philosopher, " is to act always with due regard to the fitness arising from the relations and qualities arising from causes and effects : to concur with the great and unchangeable scheme of universal felicity ; to co-operate with the general disposition and tendency of the present system of things." A kind of disquisition no more illuminating was that of Voltaire's professor of metaphysico-theologico-cosmologigology. " It is demonstrable," said he, " that things cannot be otherwise than they are ; for all being created for an end, all is necessarily for the best end. Observe that the nose has been formed to bear spectacles—thus we have spectacles." We should be wary, therefore, of attempting to draw hard and fast lines where no such lines may exist.

Nevertheless, it requires no very great penetration to discover that wherever the difference may lie there is certainly a difference, a difference so large, one may almost say, that it ceases to be a difference in degree and becomes one of kind, between a view of life such as that attributed to the Anglo-Saxons by Green (and even that of the Greeks as so acutely expounded by Mr. Lowes Dickinson in his excellent little manual), and that of the average Englishman, or for that matter Frenchman, of our own day. " Nothing but the infinite pity," said the author of " John Inglesant," " is sufficient for the infinite pathos of human life." There perhaps we have the clue to the new factor which has intervened and worked a complete transformation in man's ways of looking at himself and at the universe. The same note may be found struck again and again over the whole vast range of modern literature. We find it in Shorthouse, we find it in Maeterlinck, we find it in Robert and Elizabeth Barrett Browning, we find it in Tennyson, we find it in a writer so far apart from them all as Emile Zola.

It is true that here and there there is a revulsion, a throwback to the earlier type. Through the cosmic sea of sympathy that has flooded, as it were, the surface of the globe, the primeval fires beneath fling up now and then some reeking volcano of iron-heartedness and cynicism. This same Zola had a strong vein of it. One remembers that terrible sneer in " Dr. Pascal " ; " Suffering humanity cannot live without some lie or other to console it." Gissing too, a man in many respects poles apart from the great French realist, has that singularly sardonic remark in "Henry Rycroft": "We needs must laugh a little in the presence of suffering." Yet in his case it is rather perhaps that it is the very excess of his pity that makes him pitiless; for the phrase has an appendix, "else how should we live our lives?" In Matthew Arnold it is frequently possible without an undue exercise of fancy to detect the cynicism that is born of softness, the cruelty that is the obverse of the medal of love. "Few understood his language; none understood his aims." Thus G. H. Lewes of Goethe; and how often, indeed, do the greatest amongst us speak to us in an alien tongue that we do not comprehend? There is often a barrier, impalpable, yet none the less real, between the genius and the mass of men among whom he moves. "If," says Rousseau in his "Confessions," "I strive to speak to the people I meet, I certainly say some stupid thing to them; if I remain silent I am a misanthrope, an unsociable animal, a bear." Too true, alas!, it is that the man who wishes to attract the gaze of the "general" cannot do it by speaking frankly and freely the truth that is in him. It has been the same from the dawn of the world. "It is a kind of policy in these days," writes old Burton of the "Anatomy," "to prefix a phantastical title to a book which is to be sold: for as larks come down to a day-net, many vain readers will tarry and stand gazing, like silly passengers, at an antick picture in a painter's shop, that will not look on a judicious piece." There are those in all times who possess a fatally potent gift for thus compelling the public gaze. As Seneca so forcibly put it, "there are some who by the strangeness of their conceits will make him loiter by the way that was going to fetch a midwife for his daughter now ready to lie in." Simplicity and directness of utterance have always been recognised as a supreme merit by the few who can judge of these things. "Grandis, et ut ita dicam, pudica oratio non est maculosa, nec turgida, sed naturali pulchritudine exsurgit." Thus Petronius: but he was too much man of the world to let his practice accord with his principles.

In truth, the old materialism, whether of the more erect and admirable type or of the wallowing and grovelling type, is dead. We call ourselves materialists now, just as we call ourselves by many other strange names, but materialism no longer walks the globe. "The Animus," said Sterne, "taking up her residence, and sitting dabbling like a tadpole, all day long, both summer and winter, in a puddle, or in a liquid of any kind, how thick or thin soever, he would say, shocked his imagination." The phraseology may be paralleled from Swinburne's amusing but perhaps rather too irreverent parody of Tennyson: "The soul squats down in the body like a tinker drunk in a ditch." After all, though, we ought not perhaps to carp at the freedom of Mr. Swinburne's jesting. Was it not Erasmus, himself the prince of jesters, yet a very serious man withal, who declared in his "Encomium Moriae" that "wits have always been allowed this privilege, that they might be smart upon any transactions of life, if so that their liberty did not extend unto railing." Though he himself qualifies his judgment somewhat by his implied rebuke to Juvenal for "raking in the sink of vices to procure a laughter." Certainly, if we cannot go the whole way with those who would elevate jesting to the highest place at the feast of life, we can, nevertheless, appreciate the force of the gentle Elia's rebuke to Coleridge. "I think, Charles," remarked the poet (referring to the pulpit experiences of his earlier life), "that you never heard me preach." "My dear boy," replied Lamb, "I never heard you do anything else!" But genius is like the wind. It bloweth where it listeth. Carlyle was uttering nothing more than a much-needed warning when in "Sartor Resartus" he asked, "Would criticism erect not only finger-posts and turnpikes, but spiked gates and impassable barriers, for the mind of man?"

It may even be doubted whether at bottom all criticism is not entirely useless and purposeless. The critical spirit of Walt Whitman criticised criticism itself. "Showing the best and dividing it from the worst," runs that memorable passage in the "Song of Myself," "age vexes age; knowing the perfect fitness and equanimity of things, while they discuss I am silent, and go bathe, and admire myself." And even were all criticisms unquestionably just and impeccably acute, could they instruct any save the already instructed? "The power of instruction," observes Gibbon, "is seldom of much efficacy, except in those happy dispositions where it is already superfluous." Machiavelli was even more sweeping. "The world," says he in his placid way, "consists only of the vulgar."

# PART FOUR

# MODELS FOR PRACTICAL JOURNALISTS

## I

## THE MODEL LEADING ARTICLE

The Report of the Royal Commission on Gramophones which, as will be seen in another column, was issued last night, is bulky and complicated even when compared with previous documents of this character. It is scarcely necessary for us, we presume, to recall to the minds of our readers the circumstances which led to the Commission's appointment. To most of us they are only too painfully familiar. Suffice it to say that the ever-growing volume of public indignation on the subject of reference had by 1902 reached such a pitch that the Government of the day was compelled to yield to the pressure of opinion and appoint a Commission with the object of discovering what exactly was the present position of the law as bearing upon gramophones, and what changes, if any, were desirable. The Commissioners, who met for the first time on 9th March, 1904, were a very strong and representative body of men, amongst them being Lord Fitzgibbet, Lord Crimp, Viscount Bourton-on-the-Water (one of the greatest Speakers the House of Commons ever had), Mr. Andrew Hogmanay of the Mechanical Music Noise Abatement Society, Sir Heinrich Spitzbergen, M.P., Sir Giuseppe Piccolomini, M.P., Mr. Ivan Levinski, M.P., Lord

Julias Van Ostade, Mrs. Toop, Mr. Isaac L. Cholmondeley, the famous *entrepreneur*, Madame Coloratura, and Mr. Adolphus Jugg, of the Home Office, who acted as secretary. The first six years out of the nine over which their sittings extended were devoted to the collection of a vast body of evidence from hundreds of witnesses of every shade of opinion ; and the last two years have been spent on the preparation of the Report. Nothing could well have been more thorough than this investigation. What is the outcome of it all ? What is it that the Commission suggests should be done to diminish what is admittedly one of the most irritating of the many nuisances that harass the respectable citizen in modern England ?

The suggestions of the Commissioners—who are unanimous save as respects certain minor points in connection with which Mrs. Toop has expressed her dissent from her colleagues—may be divided into two parts : the general or positive proposals, and the particular or negative proposals. With regard to the former it will be as well to say here and now that most people will find it impossible to give them their unqualified approval. Doubtless there are some sections in this half of the Report in which the reasoning of the Commissioners is irrefragable and their conclusions unchallengeable. But at the most we can only say that this portion of the Report is, like the curate's egg, good in parts. It was inevitable that any Royal Commission which should take it upon itself to cross the Rubicon which divides the idealistic (and as we think, sound) conception of social dynamics from the purely material conception would provoke at once general and bitter indignation. It is painful to have to say this ; but it is no use blinking facts, and we think that the vast majority of the people of this country will refuse to blink them with no uncertain voice. The development of events, the process of cosmic change, has brought us to a stage where it is inevitable that we should make a choice. Nations cannot remain for ever like the proverbial donkey between the two equidistant bundles of hay ; they cannot serve two masters ; either they must love the one and hate the other or they must forsake the one and seek after the other. Much of the Labour unrest which has been of late so disquieting a feature to all stuents of social essences is directly, or at any rate indirectly, traceable to the prevailing confusion in the public mind in regard to this all-important matter. Our politicians, let us frankly admit, have given us a poor guidance in this respect. They have been in this connection but blind leaders of the blind. But it is high time that somebody should speak out.

Such are the recommendations of the Royal Commission. It is with genuine regret that we find ourselves unable to accord them our unqualified approval. That, for reasons which we have already adequately explained, is impossible. We need scarcely explain that we do not mean to convey that we put the whole of their recommendations instantly and completely out of court. On the contrary, we have little doubt but that Governments of the future will find the Report a rich storehouse from which to draw suggestions for legislation which, without making too sudden a break in the slow and orderly evolution of English institutions, will by an adjustment here and a modification there cause the whole machine to work more smoothly. That, however, is a matter with which the future will have to deal. It remains for us only to again express our sense of deep gratitude to the public-spirited men and women who by devoting so long a period to the study of one of the most grave and pressing problems that confront us to-day have set an example which every citizen would do well to follow.

## II

## THE MODEL MUSICAL CRITICISM

Last night at the Cacophonic Hall, Herr Zoppy Zqzqzqzqwich gave his last recital of the present season to an audience which filled all parts of the building. Herr Zqzqzqzqwich is not one of those, alas, too-plentiful virtuosi whose chief mission in life it is apparently to tickle the ears of the groundlings with displays of meretricious brilliancy of technique. He is an artist to the finger-tips, and, what is perhaps rarer still, a scholar. It was, therefore, in anticipation of a rich musical treat that the whole of music-loving London wended its way last night to the famous hall in Clamour Street, and it was by no means disappointed. The principal item in the great violinist's programme was Potbouille's delightful but exacting Concerto, the only example in that form that the famous Gallic leader of the Turbinistic school has yet produced, although rumour has it that he will shortly present us with another. The introductory Allegretto was played with incomparable spirit, the deftness of the player's brushwork when he came to the last rapid bars of the recurrent second theme taking the audience by storm. The same qualities were displayed in the Scherzo and the Finale ; but it was naturally in the Andante that Herr Zqzqzqzqwich was at his greatest. Both his *ton* and his *couleur* were superb ; never has that marvellously poignant fragment, which in its sorrowful yet serene wisdom seems to plumb the very depths of the human soul, been played with more convincing sanity and passion. The run of glissandic thirteenths towards the end of the movement—a thing that might well have taxed the resources of a Paganini—was negotiated with consummate ease and purity, and the sudden magic check in the triplicated barberinis at the close literally sent an almost terrible shudder over the whole of the vast audience. Needless to say, the player received a great ovation at the close.

Of Herr Zqzqzqzqwich's other numbers the most important were the familiar but ever-fresh Concerto of Beethoven and a Rhapsodie Chinoise by Mück, which had not previously been heard in this country. It is a work which it is not easy to grasp at first hearing, but there are some memorable passages in the daring young German's familiar idiom. The remaining items were Tartini's "Trille du Diable," Bach's rather saccharine "Air," and a pretty but scarcely profound "Danse des Ivrognes" by Gustave Coquetaille. The orchestral parts were sustained by the Bayswater Symphony Orchestra under Mr. James Jamieson, which also gave a stirring rendition of that gifted young English composer, Mr. Dunham Downe's "Third 'Soho' Suite."

## III

## THE MODEL COLUMN OF PERSONAL CHAT

One of the prettiest weddings of the year will be that of Lord Arthur Grandison and Miss Arabella Van Eyck Caffer, which will be celebrated at Holy Trinity, Pont Street, in the second week of next month. Holy Trinity is rapidly becoming one of the most popular churches for fashionable weddings, and there are good judges who believe that it has a future in store for it which will eclipse even the glories of St. George's, Hanover Square, in its prime. Lord Arthur, who was born in 1813, is a younger brother of the late Marquess of Stoke, of whom it used to be said that he had a family on which the sun never set, he and the Marchioness (who was a daughter of the celebrated "Billy" Dawson, of Skibbereen) having had no less than twenty-two children, most of whom, for one reason or another, went abroad to live. Lord Arthur was educated at Eton and Sandhurst, and, entering the Army, attained the rank of Major in the Royal Horse Guards (Blues); since his retirement in 1848 he has spent his time mostly between London and Glenvommit, his beautiful and picturesque place in Clackmannanshire. He is quite one of the most popular of the younger men about town.

---

The bride-to-be, who first met her prospective husband at a house party of the Countess of Bibby's in April last, was born just fifteen years ago in Newport, Long Island, where her late father, "Bunco"

Caffer, of New York, built himself one of the finest marble palaces in the Eastern States. A pretty blonde, with fascinating blue eyes and a wealth of beautiful fair hair, Miss Caffer married as her first husband Mr. Bellville P. Boyler, of Philadelphia, since when she has resumed her maiden name. Three bishops are to help tie the nuptial knot ; there are to be eighteen bridesmaids and two pages, amongst the former being the Ladies Faith, Charity, and Hope Grandison (nieces of the bridegroom), Lady Ursula Stookenham, the Hon. Peggy Rheinault (only daughter of Lord Capelcourt), Miss Lois Urquhart (youngest daughter of Urquhart of Ercildoune and Mrs. Urquhart), and three pretty cousins of the bride—the Misses Poppy Spoof, Maisie Van Eyck, and Clytemnestra Honk. The pages will be the Master of Mactavish and little Master Bartholomew Jobbe, son of the Parliamentary Secretary to the Labour Board.

---

The bride will be given away by her father, and Lord Arthur's best man will be the Earl of Torquay, who fought at his side when he went through the Pondoland campaign as personal A.D.C. to Prince Augustus of Harz-Goldenberg. Presents are pouring in on the happy couple from the friends of both families, amongst those who have sent valuable and costly gifts being H.R.H. the Crown Prince of Servia, Princess Franz Karl of Hoppe-Blichtenstein, and Count Polonyi, the eminent Hungarian statesman, whose brother not long ago married Miss Caffer's sister. The wedding dress is being made by Aglavaine, of 1864 Bond Street. It is of white Thibetan silk with a train of Coromandel suède trimmed with seed-pearls and a veil of Coan ninon. The bride's bouquet will be of arum lilies, which are becoming very popular for weddings just now, and the bridesmaids will carry tall sprays of pink excruciabilia supplied by Tibson's. The honeymoon will be spent at Boby Castle, Skye, which has been lent to the happy pair by the bridegroom's brother-in-law, the Duke of Fulham.

---

The monthly meet of the Rickshaw Club will be held (weather permitting) on Wednesday, the 23rd. Southwark Park is, as usual, the venue, and it is hoped that there will be a large turn-out, especially as the meet is the last of the present season. Amongst those who are sure to be there are Sir Guy Vaux, Lord Macgillicuddy, Viscount de Rosenheim, Mrs. Abinger-Hammer, Rear-Admiral Sir Capulet Johnstone, and Mr. " Pat " O'Connell, without whom nowadays no gathering of the kind is complete.

---

Several people have lately been seen dining at the Hotel Cordiale. Amongst those to be noticed there in the present week have been Lord Hindstairs, Mr. Ike Poppenheim, Sir Anthony Rowley, and the Marquess of Boxehill, whose little parties at the Cordiale are quite an institution.

---

Congratulations to Lord Bucklershard, who attained his majority last Thursday. Lord Bucklershard comes of a fighting stock. His maternal grandfather was the celebrated Sir Pyke Peyton, whose gallant defence of Monte Video in the earlier years of the last century earned him the commendation of the Iron Duke. His father died in one of our "little wars" on the North-West Frontier, and eight of his uncles have attained the rank of general or admiral. The young peer is expected to take a prominent part in the organisation of the Territorials in his own county. He is well blessed with this world's goods and has five historic country seats as well as a magnificent town house in Bellasis Square.

---

No less than three big dances are fixed for the 24th and many people are almost in despair about it, especially in view of the difficulty of getting young men nowadays. The dances include Lady Straphanger's, Lady Alicia Chope's, and the great ball at Ditcham House, which will have almost a semi-official character and which it is expected that royalty will honour with its presence.

---

It is officially announced that no more tickets can be issued for the Royal Parade at the Brentford Cattle Show. Since it became known that the King and Queen would both be present at this most delightful of annual functions, the Lord Chamberlain's department has been literally inundated with applications for tickets. Even as it is, the task of allocating them will be no easy matter. Whatever may be said of other State officials, nobody can deny that the Lord Chamberlain's staff certainly earn their salaries.

## IV

## THE MODEL PUZZLE CORNER

### RIDDLES

What is the difference between a schoolmaster and an engine-driver?

When is a door not a door?

What famous general never had an eye, never had a tooth, never had a leg, never had a mouth, and never had an arm, and never lost a battle?

What kind of poultry live upon Tanagra statuettes?

Why should a musician consider himself the inferior of a butcher?

What distinguished scriptural character frequently complained of neuralgia?

Where was Moses when the light went out?

### ACROSTIC

My first is in fork but not in spoon,
My second's in sun but not in moon,
My third is in planet but not in star,
My fourth is in raffle but not in bazaar,
My fifth is in donkey but not in ape,
My sixth is in form but not in shape,
My seventh's in bush not but in tree,
My whole is something you never will be.

### BURIED RIVERS

The hippopotamus is a noble beast and is much misunderstood.

I saw your Aunt Mary with a mess-jacket on.

Please immerse your hands in this refreshing water

No spectacle could be more depressing than a limp opossum.

He began gesticulating immediately he perceived me.

You had better take precisely the third turn to the right.

Oh no, said the sparrow, that will never do.

I am getting rather tired of the salmon that Uncle James will insist on sending.

SQUARE WORD

1. A river in Ecuador.
2. A certain thing you very often walk over.
3. A Jewish composer.
4. A leading daily paper.
5. A vegetable substance much used in cotton mills.
6. One of the wives of Henry the Eighth.
7. A celebrated poet recently dead.
8. A tax.

The answers to last week's puzzles have been unavoidably held over owing to the enormous mass of attempts at solution sent in. The editor hopes to be able to publish them next week with the full list of awards in connection with our great competition. In response to inquiries from " Stork " (Birchington-on-Sea) and other readers, the editor must once more make it clear that his decision is final.

to the taxpayer, and entirely out of consonance with all the best traditions of the national life."

Yesterday a meeting was held in Committee Room No. 99 of members interested in Paraguay. About twenty members of all parties were present, and it was decided that a deputation should wait upon the Prime Minister upon the subject. The matter may also be raised on the Foreign Office vote the week after next.

It is announced that the veteran Mr. Benjamin Martin, who has for so many years proved himself such an excellent chairman of committees, will not seek re-election at the next General Election. Had Mr. Martin come into the House six years earlier than he did he would have succeeded the late Sir Robert Miggleby as father of the House. It is felt that the occasion of Mr. Martin's retirement ought not to be allowed to pass by without some suitable commemoration, and a small committee has been formed, with Mr. Herbert Rogers as secretary, to organise a subscription for a presentation.

## VI

## THE MODEL ART CRITICISM

At the Haliburton Galleries, Wendover Street, Messrs. Didler have just opened an important show of oil paintings by modern Montenegrin masters. Not since 1902, the year of the memorable exhibition at the Guildhall, have we had an opportunity of seeing in London so representative a collection of works, both of the Cettinje and of the Dulcigno schools. Practically every man of note is represented by his most representative works, and the hundred odd pictures as a body will certainly convince the sceptic—if there have been any such—of the genuineness and magnitude of the Trans-Adriatic Renaissance.

Naturally one turns first to the work of M. Vlilpo Scouacho, happily still alive though no longer active, the man who above all others must be regarded as the leader and in some respects the creator of the Neo-Montenegrin movement. No less than eighteen pictures from his brush hang here—with one or two exceptions all painted in his prime. Undoubtedly the clou is "Pol Opsik, Antivari" (No. 13). Storm lours over the little port, a forlorn handful of white houses huddled between the vastness of the sea and the vastness of the mountains. Trees and waters, rocks and walls, shudder with prescience of the coming tempest; never has such an inconceivable lavishness of idea been so united with an incredible economy of means. A landscape almost equally great is "On the Skutari Road" (No. 87). The soft rays of the sunken sun gild the top of a solitary hill where foot of man has never trodden. The picture in its combined ruggedness and tenderness seems to typify the strangely blended Montenegrin character, but one doubts the advisability of the dab of Chinese white in the middle foreground. It is a picture, to return to again and again. There is an indefinable charm in all the sea pictures, in none more than in "L'Aube Consolatrice" (No. 49). Long even ripples sparkling in the full blaze of the noonday sun evenly flowing into a little beach where a grey corse lies motionless amid the wet weeds. In essence it is religious—though not in the slightest degree didactic, for didacticism in art is the abomination of desolation—in its revelation of the littleness of man and the immensity of the eternal verities. Of the other examples, "In a Sock-Suspender Factory, Monastir," is perhaps the most striking, both from the point of view of the historian of artistic development, and from that of the purely æsthetic connoisseur. The blaze of yellows and pinks and greens, the treatment of light and shade almost staggers and blinds one in its audacity; but yet how true it all is, how free from the slightest taint of triviality and commonplace; Scouacho's niche in the temple of the immortals is assured.

Scouacho's chief lieutenant, Porko Biska, died perhaps before he had reached the full maturity of his powers, but the memorable qualities in his rich, splendid, almost obstreperous art are unmistakable. Such paintings as that of a wood in autumn (76), and that of the opening of the Montenegrin

Parliament (54) roar with the wild yet intellectual orchestration of a Strauss; the force of paint could no farther go. A kindred spirit is abundantly evident in the work of his *confrère* and brother-in-law, Stunto Jokoso, who, as somebody once humorously said, sees red everywhere. More classical is the spirit of Fonio Lubar, a master of flowing and graceful line and colour. A man of whom little has previously been heard in this country is Tono Likkowich, whose symphonic landscapes, notably Nos. 22 and 49, wear a smile as mysterious and as reticent as that of Monna Lisa herself. Distinctly worthy of attention, too, is the work of Joski Protose, who is strongly under the influence of modern German realism, but brings to his work much that is distinctly his own. Of his genre pictures, "A Dead Louse" (37), for sheer ruthlessness and virility of treatment could scarcely be excelled.

In another room Messrs. Didler are exhibiting a number of water-colours of the Swedish Tyrol by Mr. J. Macdonald Barron. They are well worth a visit.

## VII

## THE MODEL COLUMN FOR HOUSEWIVES

### TWO USEFUL RECIPES

No. 1.—Take a saucepan and fill with water to the depth of two or three inches. Put it on stove and allow it to remain there until water is well on the boil. Take an egg (or two if one be deemed insufficient) and without breaking the shell place it in saucepan so that it is just covered by water. Continue to keep water on boil for three and a half or, if a somewhat denser consistency of substance be desired, four minutes. Time may be gauged with watch, clock, or sand-glass specially prepared for purpose (Messrs. Spatchcock and Wilson, of High Holborn, make excellent articles of the sort), but comparative exactitude should, if possible, be secured. At end of specified time saucepan should be briskly removed, large spoon (or fork if no spoon handy) inserted into water and egg extracted. The egg immediately after emergence from water will be seen to be wet. This, however, need cause no alarm, as water will speedily evaporate, leaving nice, clean, smooth, dry surface. Place egg in small cup of suitable shape ; serve hot and consume with salt and pepper to taste.

No. 2.—A Cheap, Easy Dish for a Large Family. Take two pounds of best Astrakhan caviare and fourteen ounces of superfine paté-de-foie-gras, and mix until a uniform paste has been secured. Take also the gizzards of eight ptarmigan and two pounds of fresh lemon pips and grind as small as possible. Boil the first mixture in butter for about twenty minutes and then add the second, stirring softly over a slow fire. When the desired softness has been obtained, drain off the water and stand aside for the steam to come off. Transfer to double saucepan and add the yolks of twelve eggs and a quarter to half a pound of guava jelly; stir and boil slowly for an hour and half. Add half-a-pint of water; allow the mixture to stand for two hours and then strain through a clean cloth. The solid remaining in the cloth may be thrown away; the liquid that comes through will, if allowed to stand for two hours, form a jelly. Place the jelly on a dish and serve with a garniture of bread-crumbs. If the utmost possible economy is necessary the bread-crumbs may be omitted.

### HOW TO OPEN A DOOR

A number of young housewives have lately informed me that they have considerable difficulty in opening doors. I cannot quite understand this, as the process is really quite a simple one. Take the handle of the door in the right hand (or the left, as the case may be) and turn slowly and without the application of unnecessary force, so that the upper portion of the handle moves from right to left (or from left to right, as the case may be), and the lower portion from left to right (or, as the case may be, from right to left). If this is done properly (unless the door is out of order, in which case the services of a locksmith should be requisitioned) the catch will be found to slip. A slight push (in some cases a pull is required, as some doors open out of a room in a different way from that in which they open into a room) must then be given and the door will then be found to yield in the manner aimed at. It may be taken as a general rule—though, like most rules, it will admit of exceptions—that a door should be shut after the opener has passed through it. Open doors frequently admit draughts, and experienced doctors will tell you that there is nothing like a draught for assisting the contraction of a cold. I have seen doors, however, which open in a different way from those above described. Each kind, of course, as is always the case in life, must be treated according to its particular nature, but the instructions I have given above will be found to be of fairly general application.

### WHAT SORT OF SHOES SHOULD BABY WEAR?

Mothers frequently have much worry and searching of hearts with respect to their babies' footwear. Babies are tender creatures and cannot in every way be treated just as we would treat grown-up persons, whose bodies and brains are alike more fully developed. To take an extreme example, nobody, for instance, would dream of putting a baby into Wellington boots. Their little feet are neither so large nor so hardened as those of their elders ; and the same thing indeed may be said of their hands. Madame Pupa, of Z6 Palmyra Buildings, Chancery Lane, has some admirable assortments of babies shoes, comfortable and hygienic in every way, which she is always glad to sell to readers who mention *The Daily Wheezer*.

## VIII

## THE MODEL CUPID'S CORNER

(*The Editress is always glad to give advice to those of her fair readers who have love or complexion troubles.*)

MARTHA (Greenwich).—No, I do not think it would be feasible or, if feasible, profitable for you to bring three Breach of Promise actions at the same time against three different men, even under the circumstances you mention. Juries are always apt to look at these matters from the male point of view; and, after all, you have been a little fickle in your affections, haven't you?

ROSIE B. (Newcastle-on-Tyne).—Yes, your position does seem to be a rather cruel one. You say that you are quite certain he loves you; and yet somehow I feel that if he really loves you as much as he says he does, he ought to be willing to give up the garlic. Try what a little quiet persuasion will do, dear; endeavour to make him see matters more from your point of view. God has given us women a great gift in the power of our tongues. If you find him still obdurate, let me hear from you again.

LILY OF THE VALLEY (Seven Dials).—Your complaint sounds like eczema. It is very hard to get rid of it The best cream for it that I know is prepared by Madame Scheherazade, of Bond Street, whose advertisement will be found in another column.

COON (Portarlington)—You are a very foolish

girl, Coon, and I am very much ashamed of you. I should have thought that at this time of day everybody would have known that tight-lacing is one of the very worst things from the point of view of physical well-being. The girl who, as you say you have done, brings her waist down to seven inches, is committing a crime against society. But there, I suppose I am very old-fashioned.

DISTRACTED TEACHER (Exeter).—Yes, he has behaved very, very badly indeed, and I must say that in your position I should find it very, very hard to forgive a man who had behaved in such a manner. I do not think you did wisely in refraining from reproaching him when you found out that he was meeting your friend and you on alternate Saturday afternoons and taking her to stalls at the theatre when he only took you to a beggarly cinematograph show. In my opinion you should have gone straight to his mother and told her outright what you thought of her son. Depend on it, my dear, a man who will "carry on" like this is not worth thinking about. I am sure he would never make a good husband.

POPPY (Stornoway).—I think you have acted hastily, Poppy. To attempt to attach a man by leading strings is the worst mistake a woman can make. You say that he cut you in the street when he was walking out with another young lady. Well, what if he did? He may have had very good reason; and in any case you ought to have afforded him an opportunity of giving an explanation before sending him a letter of the sort that you enclose. If only young people would be more tolerant of each other's little ways, the world would be a much happier place than it is. I think, Poppy, that you will learn that when you are a year or two older.

MABEL (Bettws-y-Coed).—No ; most emphatically no !

JUNIPER (London).—Asafœtida is an excellent thing for it and also very pleasant to take.